Excellence
in
First-Year Writing
2017/2018

The English Department Writing Program
and
The Gayle Morris Sweetland Center for Writing

Edited by
Dana Nichols

Published in 2018 by Michigan Publishing
University of Michigan Library

© 2018 Gayle Morris Sweetland Center for Writing

Permission is required to reproduce material from this title in other
publications, coursepacks, electronic products, and other media.

Please send permission requests to:

Michigan Publishing
1210 Buhr Building
839 Greene Street
Ann Arbor, MI 48104
lib.pod@umich.edu

ISBN 978-1-60785-490-6

Table of Contents

Excellence in First-Year Writing

Excellence in First-Year Writing 2017/2018

EDWP Writing Prize Chairs

Kyle Frisina

Lizzie Hutton

EDWP Writing Prize Committee

Alena Aniskiewicz

Annette Beauchamp

Megan Behrend

Annie Bolotin

Aaron Burch

Catherine Cassel

Rachel Cawkwell

Dory Fox

Michael Hinken

Katherine Hummel

Ruth Li

Olivia Ordonez

Adrienne Raw

Ali Shapiro

Sweetland Writing Prize Chair

Dana Nichols

Sweetland Writing Prize Committee

Angie Berkley

Jimmy Brancho

Cat Cassel

Raymond McDaniel

Dana Nichols

Carol Tell

Sweetland Writing Prize Judges

Scott Beal

Louis Cicciarelli

Lillian Li

Shuwen Li

Christine Modey

Simone Sessolo

Naomi Silver

Administrative Support

Laura Schulyer

Aaron Valdez

Winners List

Feinberg Family Prize for Excellence in First-Year Writing

Adam Kamps "Suffering and Sympathy: The Role of Suffering and Self-Restriction in Hawthorne's Works"
Nominated by Lazarus Belle, English 124

Bennett Hendricks, "The Curtain"
Nominated by Mindy Misener, English 125

Sydnie Boulé, "Our Disappearing Shorelines"
Nominated by Catherine Fairfield, English 125

Matt Kelley/Granader Family Prize for Excellence in First-Year Writing

Wisteria Deng, "Six Reasons"
Nominated by Leslie Stainton, LHSP 125

Zofia Ferki, "As Time Ticks By"
Nominated by Leslie Stainton, LHSP 125

Granader Family Prize for Excellence in Multilingual Writing

Pok Yu Chan, "Comparative Analysis of Two Culturally Distinct Texts: Snickers Got You Snickering"
Nominated by Scott Beal, Writing 120

Dorcas Li, "Hey, Where are You?"
Nominated by Scott Beal, Writing 120

Granader Family Prize for Outstanding Writing Portfolio

Rita Hathaway, "The Spectrum Center: Enriching the Campus Experience"
Nominated by Simone Sessolo, Writing 100

Ying-Hsuan Wu, "Past/Future of My Home"
Nominated by Jimmy Brancho, Writing 100

Feinberg Family Prize nominees

Student Name	Instructor Name
Ayodele Adelaja	April Conway
Ayush Arora	Cat Cassel
Hanisha Arora	Franny Choi
Jad Baki	Cat Cassel
Michael Berg	Annette Beauchamp
Anne Bonds	Rebecca Hixon
Sydnie Boulé	Catherine Fairfield
Angelina Brede	Aaron Burch
Grant Buchmiller	Kelly Wheeler
Lucy Carpenter	Aaron Burch
Britney Cheng	Annette Beauchamp
Anna Dang	Rachel Cawkwell
Meredith Days	Kathryne Bevilacqua
Alisha Dhallan	Adelay Elizabeth Witherite
Kara Dickinson	Michelle May-Curry
Julia Doskoch	Franny Choi
Akili Echols	Kathryne Bevilacqua
Ari Esrig	Aaron Burch
Jacob Feuerborn	Patricia Khleif
Gabrielle Flint	Mindy Misener
Helen Foldenauer	Elizabeth Dickey
Jordan Goodrich	April Conway
Melissa Grembi	Annette Beauchamp
Marit Gulbrandson	Katherine Hummel
Stephanie Guralnick	Mindy Misener
Ellen Hadley	Katherine Hummel
Arman Haveric	Megan Behrend
Anna He	Aaron Burch

Feinberg Family Prize nominees (con't)

Student Name	Instructor Name
Bennett Hendricks	Mindy Misener
Matthew Hoenig	April Conway
Simone Jaroslaw	Molly Keran
Kaitlin Kahler	Rebecca Hixon
Charles (Charlie) Kamper	Tiffany Ball
Adam Kamps	Lazarus Belle
Ivana Khreizat	Aaron Burch
Ryan Kimball	April Conway
Griffin Klaft	Aaron Burch
Sydney Knoll	Jacqueline Larios
Jack Kuczmanksi	Tricia Khleif
Jason Lansing	Annika Pattenaude
Shangbo Liao	Annette Beauchamp
Senna Lim	Rachel Cawkwell
Minxin (Maisie) Liu	Adelay Elizabeth Witherite
Christina Losee	Kelly Wheeler
Ashley Mark	Cat Cassel
Natalie McMyn	Rachel Cawkwell
Taylor Mitchell	Mike Hinken
Abigail Muro	Elizabeth Dickey
Ryan Nelson	Franny Choi
Yulia Odinokova	Molly Keran
Rahil Patel	Annette Beauchamp
Shivangi Patel	April Conway
Jack Pennington	Matt Bellamy
Vedhika Raghunathan	Annette Beauchamp
Mark Ricciardi	Mike Hinken
Hunter Rice	Mike Hinken

Feinberg Family Prize nominees (con't)

Student Name	Instructor Name
Ally Rigney	Rachel Cawkwell
Melanie Rogers	Molly Keran
Maddie Ross	Mike Hinken
Conrad Sager	Matt Bellamy
Alexis Schachter	Dory Fox
Annabel (Annie) Schnoll	Tiffany Ball
Jack Silberman	Michelle May-Curry
Emma Singleton	Aaron Burch
Madison Stewart	Cat Cassel
Matthew Tarry	Kathryne Bevilacqua
Maxine Taskin	Franny Choi
Emily Tumminia	Jacqueline Larios
Ninochtka Valdez	Kelly Wheeler
Alexander Vidinas	Annie Bolotin
Marc Warren	Mi Jin Christina Kim
Garrett Wilson	Tiffany Ball
Karli Wulwick	Aaron Burch
Usha Yeruva	Katherine Hummel
Jiazhen Yang	April Conway
Annika Zdon	Cat Cassel
Ruixi (Grace) Zhang	Adelay Elizabeth Witherite
Fei Zhou	Franny Choi

Matt Kelley/Granader Family Prize nominees

Student Name	Instructor Name
Basil AlSubee	Veronica Stanich
Brendan Baker	Sophie Hunt
Alycia Bird	Sahin Acikgoz
Davis Boos	Christopher Matthews
Malcolm Broda	Johanna Folland
Allison Burns	Scott Beal
Phoebe Danaher	Susan Walton
Joshua Degraff	Frederick Peters
Wisteria Deng	Leslie Stainton
Fareah Fysudeen	Vedran Catovic
Zofia Ferki	Leslie Stainton
Catherine Garton	Adrienne Jacaruso
Bellina Gaskey	Carol Tell
Katyanna Guthrie	Sophie Hunt
Joshua Hartman	Grace Zanotti
Charissa Hasper	Laura Hirshfield
Grace Hermann	Susan Walton
Rahul Kak	Harry Kashdan
Miri Kim	Harry Kashdan
Sofia Kruszka	Daniel Diffendale
Jennifer Lange	Scott Beal
Lily Lima	Scott De Orio
Christy Ly	Grace Zanotti
Margaret Miron	Christopher Matthews

Matt Kelley/Granader Family Prize nominees (con't)

Student Name	Instructor Name
Leila Mullison	Laura Hirshfield
Abha Panda	Daniel Diffendale
Sarah Perrigo	Sahin Acikgoz
Micah Pollens-Dempsey	Carrie Wood
Estrella Salgado	Simone Prince-Eichner
Abby Schneider	Catherine Brown
Jonathon Spunar	Donald Sells
Gisselle Zuniga	Johanna Folland

Granader Family Portfolio Prize nominees

Student Name	Instructor Name
Tyler Bentley	Julie Babcock
Alec Cohen	Cat Cassel
Mary Finch	Elizabeth Dickey
Rita Hathaway	Simone Sessolo
Sarah Pyykkonen	Elizabeth Dickey
Amelia Montgomery	Scott Beal
Emma Revelant	Simone Sessolo
Benjamin St-Juste	Scott Beal
Ying-Hsuan Wu	James Brancho

Granader Family Multilingual Prize nominees

Student Name	Instructor Name
Hyung Jun (Henry) Baik	Shuwen Li
Pok Yu Chan	Scott Beal
Jee Yol Chung	Scott Beal
Dorcas Li	Scott Beal
Yicheng (Jason) Liu	Shuwen Li
Xian (Winston) Wu	Shuwen Li

Introduction

First-year writing is a foundational course. Offered at the University of Michigan and at virtually every other college and university in this nation, this course introduces students to the intellectual life of higher education. It also introduces students to the writing that will be expected of them during their undergraduate years. On this campus, students in first-year writing courses produce 25-30 pages of polished writing, or writing that has been thoroughly revised and edited. First-year writing also introduces students to the social nature of writing by giving them opportunities to participate in peer review, receive feedback from Sweetland's Peer Consultants, and meet with their instructors and/or faculty in Writing Workshop.

Students at UM can take their first-year writing course in many different departments and programs: Classical Studies, Comparative Literature, English, History, Honors, Slavic, and Residential College all offer first-year writing courses. So at the same time that they are being introduced to college writing, students also have an opportunity to learn about a specific discipline. Regardless of where they complete their first-year writing course, students meet the same general requirements, and all versions of the course emphasize evidence-based argument. Together, all of these features give student writers a solid foundation to build on as they move through their undergraduate years.

This book contains a sampling of some of the best writing produced in first-year writing classes during the past year. Instructors of first-year writing courses nominated students whose writing impressed them as exemplifying exceptional quality, and faculty judges undertook the difficult job of identifying winning selections. We can all learn a great deal from this collection of writing nurtured by instructors and drafted, revised, and polished by students.

Dana Nichols deserves many thanks for editing this entire collection, as does Aaron Valdez for creating an attractive design for this book. Members of the Sweetland Writing Prize Committee were Angie Berkley, Jimmy Brancho, Cat Cassel, Raymond McDaniel, Dana Nichols, and Carol Tell. Judges for the Matt Kelly/Granader Family Prize for first-year writing were Scott Beal, Louis Cicciarelli, Lillian Li, Christine Modey, Simone Sessolo, and Naomi Silver. We are indebted to these faculty members for their thoughtful work.

The judging for the Feinberg Family English Department Writing Program Prizes in Analytical Argument, Narrative Argument and Research-based Argument was overseen by Graduate Student Mentors Kyle Frisina and Lizzie Hutton. The judges were Alena Aniskiewicz, Annette Beauchamp, Megan Behrend, Annie Bolotin, Aaron Burch, Cat Cassel, Rachel Cawkwell, Dory Fox, Michael Hinken, Katherine Hummel, Ruth Li, Olivia Ordonez, Adrienne Raw, and Ali Shapiro. Comprising both lecturers and graduate student instructors from the English Department Writing Program, these judges were extremely generous with the time they volunteered on behalf of these contests.

Special thanks are due to the many instructors who provided foundational learning experiences for their students, encouraged them to take up new ways of writing, and identified them as outstanding writers.

Most important, of course, are all the students who submitted essays for these winning prizes. Many of these students took risks by stepping away from what they had learned in high school, by trying new genres and difficult topics, and by sharing their drafts with relative strangers. These students guarantee the ongoing vitality and importance of writing on this campus.

Anne Ruggles Gere, Director, Sweetland Center for Writing
Megan Sweeney, Director, English Department Writing Program

Feinberg Family Prize for Excellence in First-Year Writing

We are so pleased to introduce these essays for the Feinberg Family Prize for Excellence in First Year Writing. The close to one hundred essays nominated for this prize demonstrate the lively passion and exceptional rhetorical skill possessed by University of Michigan first-year writing students. We congratulate all those nominated as well as the winners whose essays are included here.

In addition, we congratulate the instructors of the writers nominated for these prizes. We would also like to highlight the fact that nominated essays blossomed through conversation with peers. A cornerstone of the English Department Writing Program, after all, is students' engagement with small group workshops and peer critiques. Here, student writers learn to honor each other's writing by giving it their close and generous attention, and to develop the confidence to take constructive criticism with the seriousness that it deserves.

One of our hopes is that these essays can serve as models and inspiration for future students in writing courses across the university. Yet another hope is that these essays be understood as evidence of what our first-year writing program and its courses successfully achieve. Led by devoted instructors, these courses inspire sustained forms of attentiveness and purpose-driven inquiry, inviting students to learn about the world around them through the challenging act of putting words on the page. EDWP's first-year courses teach students how genres work, what constitutes persuasive argument, and the extent to which different audiences--not to mention different aims--require different approaches to structure, evidence, and tone. Students' heightened awareness of these elements of discourse prepares them for richer participation in conversations elsewhere: in other classrooms, across the university, and throughout the many spheres in which they travel.

The three winning essays reflect a shared desire on the part of our university's undergraduate writers to grapple with urgent contemporary questions--in this case regarding belief, suffering, and responsibility to oneself and the world. Inspired by a diverse set of provocations, these essays demonstrate thoughtful investment at the levels of both content and form in the varied ways language can function: to persuade, to warn, to remember, to connect. These essays--together with the other exceptional work nominated for these prizes--remind us that strong writing can impact its readers in ways an author might never have imagined when first beginning to compose.

Kyle Frisina & Lizzie Hutton
Graduate Student Mentors, English Department Writing Program

Suffering and Sympathy: The Role of Suffering and Self-Restriction in Hawthorne's Works

by Adam Kamps
From English 124
Nominated by Lazarus Belle

Adam penned this compelling essay in English 124, though on first read it seemed as if it came from a more advanced course. The prompt was deliberately open-ended, and Adam took this opportunity to analyze the affective dimensions of suffering and sympathy in two of Nathaniel Hawthorne's more difficult texts, *The Scarlet Letter* and the short story "The Celestial Railroad." Though these are radically different texts, Adam expertly weaves them together, crafting an insightful examination of Hawthorne's complicated relationship with New England's Puritan heritage and the function of emotional tribulation in the formation of character. The essay is impressive for its intellectual maturity, its masterful command of language, its appreciation of the cultural precedents of the texts, and—without a hint of moralizing or speculation—its ability to unpack complex themes of sin, guilt, and redemption. Perhaps this essay's greatest virtue is its willingness to eschew simplistic arguments in favor of complexity and ambiguity, to leave us resting—as do the works of Hawthorne themselves—in spaces of apparently irreconcilable morality, in the grey spaces our very human feelings sometimes leave us in.

As educators of young writers, I think we look forward to essays that turn the tables on us, as it were, leaving us feeling for the moment like we're the ones who are learning. Adam's essay is certainly one of this kind and, for my part, it has changed the way I think about these texts and the way I will teach them in the future.

Lazarus Belle

Suffering and Sympathy: The Role of Suffering and Self-Restriction in Hawthorne's Works

Puritan life is often typified in modern understanding by its strict adherence to a self-denying religiosity and an austere asceticism. These practices are by no means singularly associated with Puritanism, existing as integral aspects of early Catholicism and many other Christian and non-Christian faiths; however, the modern American may find the Puritan understanding of suffering and self-denial particularly relevant because of the vestigial effects of these early-American convictions. Nathaniel Hawthorne, an author whose connection with these matters was genealogical, concerned two of his works with the concepts of avoidable suffering and self-denial. What purpose can suffering serve? What are the dangers of ease? Does one's will need to be abnegated for one to act rightly? Hawthorne, in his works *The Scarlet Letter* and "The Celestial Railroad," situates these themes within a Puritan town and the satirized landscape of John Bunyan's *The Pilgrim's Progress*, an allegory concerned with the benefits of suffering. In these works, Nathaniel Hawthorne advocates the benefits of suffering, as they relate to the repentance of the sufferer and the development of their sympathies, while contesting the ineffectual, alienating introspection of the Puritans by explaining how human action can be both beneficial and guiltlessly joyful.

Firstly, Hawthorne addresses the function of suffering in "The Celestial Railroad." "The Celestial Railroad" is a satire which utilizes the landscape of John Bunyan's *The Pilgrim's Progress* to criticize the naively melioristic practices of Hawthorne's contemporary generation. *The Pilgrim's Progress* is an allegory, relating the trials of a pilgrimage to the adversities that Christians must overcome in their lives. The satirical nature of Hawthorne's piece lies in the absurd intrusion of modern conveniences into a pilgrimage that had formerly been characterized by great suffering and righteous endurance. Those in the work who take advantage of these conveniences are condemned to Hell, provoking this question: What is it about the arduous journey of the pilgrim that renders them better off than had they taken an easier path? As the passengers travel through Hell, Mr. Smooth-it-away, the conductor, quells their anxieties concerning the ominous scene that confronts them by explaining that they are simply travelling through a half-extinct volcano. The speaker remarks that anyone who had witnessed the sight "would have seized upon Mr. Smooth-it-away's comfortable explanation as greedily as we did" (192). When this passage is considered with the speaker's destination in mind, it is clear that Hawthorne is making a point about the human proclivity to suspend incredulity for the sake of adopting more comfortable, palatable outlooks.

But why are those who take the train unable to acknowledge threatening circumstances? Does good thinking necessarily involve a form of suffering or self-denial? If so, how does that suffering bring about a change in outlook? In *The Pilgrim's Progress*, pilgrims must travel with their baggage (the weight of their sins) until the weights become too unbearable, at which point Christ removes them. The speaker in "The Celestial Railroad" states that "Our enormous burdens, instead of being carried on our shoulders…were all snuggly deposited in the baggage car" (187). The passengers lack a fundamental understanding of the purpose of burdens. The pilgrims on the train are never truly relieved of their sin because they never feel the weight of their sin. In "The Celestial Railroad," Hawthorne criticizes the progressive aversion towards suffering that characterized his contemporary generation of thinkers, by showing how the willful negligence of these experiences affects the ability of the would-be sufferer to see the world as it is. He establishes a relationship between suffering and the recognition/avoidance of sin, implying that suffering forces individuals to consider their sin, thereby urging them to repent of it.

In *The Scarlet Letter*, Hawthorne complicates this relationship between repentance and suffering, acknowledging that not all suffering is effective towards instruction. He does this through his character Dimmesdale, a man who has sinned, but who does not feel that he has truly repented because he has not made that sin public. Dimmesdale seems to think that he must pay for his sin by suffering. He whips himself with a "bloody scourge" and fasts "until his knees tremble beneath him" (99). He is punitively introspective, dwelling on the conflict between his role in the church and his hidden sin. Neither of these sufferings, physical or mental, bring him true relief. "The Celestial Railroad" reflects Hawthorne's belief about how faithful endurance of suffering can move the pilgrim from a place of complacency to an awareness of truth; however, in the case of Dimmesdale, he suffers for seven years and is still "powerless even to repent" (136). What is the difference between Dimmesdale's suffering and the faithful pilgrim's suffering? When travelling through the Valley of the Shadow of Death, the narrator of "The Celestial Railroad" says that "all through the Dark Valley I was tormented, pestered, and dolefully bewildered" by expressions of his own sins and evil passions (194). Instead of bringing about change in him, these sufferings push the narrator into further denial of his sinful nature. This passage suggests that there can be an incorrect way to suffer –a wrong way of interpreting misery. Like the narrator of "The Celestial Railroad," Dimmesdale suffers but is unable to accept the truth conveyed by his misery—that he must be honest with his parishioners about his adultery. Is there something wrong with Dimmesdale's character that renders suffering unable to produce its intended effect? Or is there something wrong with the suffering that he subjects himself too?

In his essay "*The Scarlet Letter* as a Dialectic of Temperament and Idea," Robert Stanton affirms both questions, arguing that ineffectual suffering is always the result of a misalignment between a human's temperament and their particular misery. Stanton believes that Dimmesdale, a cowardly yet prideful man, submits himself to an ineffectual form of suffering even though he knows how to truly repent. Stanton believes that Hawthorne critiques Puritan asceticism, through the example of Dimmesdale, implying that Puritan introspection/suffering is treated as an end in and of itself rather than a means to an end. Perhaps introspection cannot function as penitence, but Hawthorne is not saying that suffering has no intrinsic value as it relates to absolution. During their meeting in the forest, Hester asks Dimmesdale whether the sufferings of his past seven years have been enough penitence. He responds "Of penance I have had enough! Of penitence there has been none" (131). Dimmesdale's daughter, Pearl, has "a bitter scorn of many things, which, when examined, might be found to have the taint of falsehood in them" (123). When she happens upon Dimmesdale punishing himself by simulating his own public confession during the night, when no one watches, she asks him if he would "stand here with mother and me, to-morrow noontide?" (105). Pearl's contempt for dishonesty is pertinent to Hawthorne's understanding of repentance when considered alongside her role as the vessel of "justice and retribution" (123). Dimmesdale is only removed from under the Devil's "burning finger" when he confesses his sin before his congregation, but his disclosure is not only valuable in its communication of hidden truth (174). Despite what Stanton's interpretation may suggest, there is a justice in Dimmesdale's suffering. Pearl's insistence that he stand alongside her and her mother suggests that Hester and Dimmesdale's differential experience of public ignominy is unjust, and that Dimmesdale must suffer in order for there to be justice. Hawthorne disavows the fruitless introspective suffering of the Puritans; however, he believes that suffering can still be required as a means of penitence.

Hawthorne recognizes the benefits that certain forms of suffering can confer, but how does he view the suffering that is denying one's nature or one's happiness? Is this form of suffering fruitful? These answers are found in a close analysis of Hester, and her connection to her daughter Pearl. Hester's relationship to the restraint of her freedoms is irregular. She complies as much as she defies. She wears the mark of her shame but has embroidered it with "fine red cloth" and "fantastic flourishes of gold thread" (37). She has undertaken no "genuine and steadfast penitence, but something doubtful" that "might be deeply wrong" (57). Though she escapes New England and the control of the Puritans, she returns to that house between nature and Puritan society, between self-law and the regiment of social mores. Robert Stanton argues that this unsettled conflict between Hester's temperament and religious stricture is a portrayal of the incompatibility of self-reliance and a life lived in a coordination with society.

However, the example of Pearl suggests something quite different. Pearl, Hester's daughter, the "effluence of her mother's passions," lives her life with an untethered freedom (113). She laughs in the face of austere Puritanism. Throughout the romance, Pearl is equated with nature and described as a bird or an elf like those left behind in England. What does Hawthorne mean by creating a character so adverse to the denial of her passions? Is this character, who is "a law unto herself" (92), meant to be interpreted prescriptively? Or is there some other purpose for Pearl's inclusion in this work? During the procession for the appointment of Salem's new governor, the speaker describes the festivities of England and draws them into sharp contrast with the feigned merriment of the Puritans. The speaker remarks that even generations after the Puritans, "We have yet to learn again the forgotten art of gaiety" (159). This text throws new light on Pearl's association with England and her behavior, which perpetually contradicts Puritan expectations. Hawthorne has shown that the Puritan form of self-denial unnecessarily hampers people's joy. But why does he make Pearl as unmanageable as she is? Does he not believe that human will should in any way be tempered? The speaker describes the scene of Dimmesdale's ignominy as breaking a spell in his daughter, Pearl. Suffering to watch her father's shame "developed all of her sympathies…she would grow up amid human joy and sorrow, nor for ever do battle with the world, but be a woman in it" (175). Hawthorne does not say that because of her suffering, Pearl learns to deny her longings and live a moral life. Instead of Pearl's freedom being denied her, her impish, antagonistic temperament matures, and she develops new sympathies, which will help her to use that freedom in a way that more often benefits others. For the same reason that Hester comforts and counsels the "wounded, wasted, wronged, misplace or erring" (180) women in her community and that Dimmesdale's sermons strike such a cord with his parishioners, Pearl's sufferings bring her into the human sphere, allowing her to empathize with other sufferers.

Hester's character is sympathetic to others, to an extent, yet she cannot be unconstrained in her actions because of her previous sins and the way that they have tainted her. During the meeting of Hester and Dimmesdale in the forest, the speaker says that "the breach which guilt has once made into the human soul is never, in this mortal state, repaired" (138). During the same scene, Hester throws her letter off, and it seems that she would be a law unto herself, as she was before. Instead, Pearl keeps her mother honest, and requires her to place it back on her breast. Since Hester has sinned, her "citadel" of defense against the enemy has been breached. "There is still the ruined wall, and near it the stealthy tread of the foe that would win over again" (138). Hester cannot act according to her nature because, in giving herself over to her passions, she would sin again. Unlike Pearl, whose character has become attuned to the needs of others and can therefore rely on her own good will, Hester will forever be stained by her guilt. Unlike Dimmesdale, who also sinned, her suffering has not moved her to repentance, but instead has made her an inhabitant of "another sphere," "terror and repugnance" being her "sole portion in the universal heart" (58). Hester's shaming is an example of suffering applied in discordance with temperament. Instead of bringing her to repentance, her public ignominy turns an already strong-willed woman into a sour and obstinate one. In her youth, Hester "imagined that she herself might be the destined prophetess," to establish the roles of women and men on more equal ground, but in her old age she recognizes that this mission cannot be "confided to a woman…bowed down with shame, and wise…through dusky grief" (180).

At a more liminal moment in American History, when the meliorism of transcendentalists and free-thinkers began to threaten the influence of a self-abnegating Puritanism, Nathaniel Hawthorne saw something to be lost in the avoidance of suffering, while also recognizing the continuing influence of its more ineffectual instantiations. In his works, "The Celestial Railroad" and *The Scarlet Letter*, Hawthorne hems in the Puritanical perception of suffering, admitting that in some cases suffering can aid repentance, but adding also that suffering is too often administered unsuccessfully in that regard. While Hawthorne does not seek to fence in human will by instructing humans to live in denial of their passions, he understands that suffering is often necessary to develop people's sympathies, and to bring their will into alignment with the wills of others. Nathaniel Hawthorne uses the austere setting of Puritan life to communicate that human agency and good action can coexist, but not without the corrective force of suffering.

Works Cited

Bunyan, John. *Pilgrim's Progress*. Aneko Press, 2014.

Hawthorne, Nathaniel. *The Celestial Railroad and Other Stories*. Penguin, 1963.

Hawthorne, Nathaniel. *The Scarlet Letter*. Dover Publications, 1994.

Stanton, Robert. "'The Scarlet Letter' as Dialectic of Temperament and
Idea." *Studies in the Novel*, vol. 2, no. 4, 1970, pp. 474–486., www.jstor.org/stable/29531426.

The Curtain

by Bennett Hendricks
From English 125
Nominated by Mindy Misener

In a pre-writing exercise for this essay, Bennett asked, "How could a legitimate medical professor who taught at Columbia turn into a TV star who feeds on the sale of ambiguous and non-scientific medical practices?" Real, honest questions are risky, and Bennett's perspicacious essay shows us what the payoff can be.

The challenge—and, dare I say, the joy—of crafting a research-based argument lies in articulating what is essentially a story about how your sources speak to each other, why their voices matter when taken together, and how your readers ought to think about the subject they address. Bennett's work is an excellent example of this kind of artistic control: his essay layers sources to construct an understanding of Dr. Oz that grows more complex as we read. Fortunately, Bennett doesn't try to resolve this complexity. Instead, he steers the end of the essay into a dramatic turn that is, in effect, a vigorous, unnerving answer to the question Why does it matter?

I don't want to spoil the essay's conclusion, so I'll simply say this: that the essay's full answer to this additional question came quite late in the drafting process -- proof (as if we needed more of it) that time and a commitment to the slow growth of ideas are essential to exceptional writing.

Mindy Misener

The Curtain

Imagine the dreaded Disney World wait-time ordeal, except substitute "It's a Small World" with the Research Medical Center in Kansas City. The belly of the building fails to accommodate the hoard, whose tail snakes down the sidewalk. With palpable anticipation, the amorphous mass of women coagulates around the entrance. It's still dark. A camera crew approaches, setting up camp to capture his arrival. Dr. Mehmet Oz gracefully steps out of the back seat of his sedan to a joyous reception. His stethoscope complements his pale blue scrubs. His tamed helmet of hair complements his gaunt, fifty-two-year-old face. Lights! Camera! Action! A skilled showman, he works the adoring crowd, engaging his followers to the camera's delight. He's in his element. The women effuse gratitude and praise. Many do not have medical insurance and have not seen a doctor in years. A portion made its exodus simply to behold the medical prophet in the flesh. As the multitudes flock into the hospital to receive free medical screening, a few women are graced with conversation. "I haven't seen a doctor in eight years. I'm scared. You're the only one I trust," one woman pours out. Oz's hand lands gently on her shoulder. "I'll see you inside. We are going to get you through this, and we'll do it together." Scene.

Dr. Oz is arguably America's most influential doctor. He draws a daily audience of four million viewers on *The Dr. Oz Show*. Oprah Winfrey dubbed him "America's Doctor" in 2004 after giving him his start as a TV personality. He hasn't looked back. Dr. Oz, telegenic and eloquent, seems to be made for TV stardom. It comes as a surprise, then, that Oz boasts such a high-caliber résumé. A 1982 Harvard graduate, he went on to acquire joint M.B.A and medical degrees from the University of Pennsylvania. For four consecutive years he received the prestigious Blakemore Research Award as a medical resident at Columbia. For more than 20 years, Oz served as professor in the department of surgery at Columbia. Currently he specializes in heart transplants at the esteemed New York-Presbyterian Hospital, where he performs surgeries every Thursday. Viewing

Oz's character through the lens of his pedigree only offers surface-level insight, however. This writing aims to take an x-ray machine to his inner man. Oz's pre-examination shows an already heightened susceptibility to the disease of post-truth complicity (Belluz; Specter, "The Operator").

Oz firmly adheres to the belief that western medical philosophy is incomplete. Dr. Oz describes western medicine as reductive, focusing on illness versus health. In the same vein, Oz is a sincere proponent of alternative medical practices. He holds a genuine, long-held interest in this area, and wields his massive influence as "America's Doctor" to advance his platform of alternative medicine. To his audience, Oz's holistic view of medical care is a much-needed alternative to the dominance of big pharmaceutical companies. Oz himself says he longs for the days when "our ancestors lived in small villages and there was always a healer in that village" (Specter, "The Operator"). Oz appears to be a righteous crusader in the medical field. His holistic view of medicine seems noble:

> Western medicine has a firm belief that studying human beings is like studying bacteria in petri dishes. Doctors do not want questions from their patients; it's easier to tell them what to do than to listen to what they say. But people are on a serpentine path through life, and that is the way it is supposed to be. All I am trying to do is put a couple of road signs out there. I sit on that set every day, and that is what I am focussing on. The road signs (Spector, "Columbia").

The thought that simple, safe, natural precautionary measures can reliably thwart common illness, coupled with the notion that the American medical system routinely subverts natural remedies to line pockets, entices Oz's followers. For this reason, it is not surprising that Oz wields the status of cult leader among his base. This cult of personality, and the reality that alternative medicine regularly toes the line between fact and fiction, complicates the figure of Dr. Oz. This man crafted his image into that of a family doctor: offering hope, respecting faith, suggesting diet, gently nudging for more exercise. While playing this persona Oz secretly tugs on the primal response of fear in his audience, the fear that they are being lied to everywhere else. Oz's present TV personality may be best characterized as a true wolf in sheep's clothing.

Oz's upbringing must be analyzed to further unbox his psyche. The drive to win, first and foremost, defined Mehmet Oz's childhood. Oz's father, Mustafa Oz, instilled in him this mindset at a young age. Oz shares, "The only question my father ever asked me was: Did anyone do better than you?" Mustafa Oz, a Turkish thoracic surgeon who immigrated to the US in the 1950's, believed in work ethic above all else. His parenting style points to Mehmet's acquired penchant for success. With life framed as a competition, Mehmet gained a strong internal appetite for achievement. This, in part, helps to explain his exceptional resume and his competitive nature. "If I came home, proud and excited, with a ninety-seven on an exam, he would ask if somebody got a higher grade," Oz says, "and if George or Tom got a ninety-eight then I might as well have failed. When I made all-state football, which was a big deal for me, he didn't ask me what it was or comment on it. He thought sports were a distraction. When his friends congratulated him at work the next day, he didn't know what they were talking about" (Spector, "The Operator"). The latter subject, I suspect, reveals a key aspect of Mehmet's bent towards TV stardom. With his life framed around pleasing his father, it must have stung badly when he did not receive any recognition for his All-State title. Not only did Mehmet gain the desire to win, he experienced the dissatisfaction of not being recognized for it. Michael Specter's article containing an interview of Dr. Eric Rose illuminates Oz's appetite for admiration. Oz served on Rose's heart transplant team at a time when anti-rejection drugs were beginning to make heart transplants more common, and thus receive less publicity. Specter recounts the circumstances: "On October 25, 1996, Frank Torre, the brother of the New York Yankees manager Joe Torre, received a new heart at New York-Presbyterian... The transplant, which was a success, took place during that year's World Series." The operation attracted significant attention in the news cycle: "a collage of articles about the event— "*Heart of the Yankees*" the Daily News offered, in supersize type—still hangs in the cardiac-department offices at New York-

Presbyterian." Rose says that while the publicity was good for him and for New York-Presbyterian Hospital, he "learned that it wasn't something [he] enjoyed." When asked about Oz's reaction though, Rose observes that the experience "was [Oz's] first big splash of publicity, and he loved it." Rose then speculates that the experience likely propelled Oz toward his current career ("The Operator").

Long before the manifestation of his TV personality, Mehmet Oz felt an authentic calling to surgery. Speaking to Michael Specter, Oz shares about a formative moment shadowing his father in the workplace:

> I still remember vividly going on rounds with him, and once seeing him take an eighteen-gauge needle and plunge it into a guy who was dying of pneumonia, injecting saline right into his trachea, which got him to cough up the plug that was choking him. It made me think I'd love to be able to do that ("The Operator").

Compelled by a calculated cockiness, a surgeon's conviction is this: cracking a sternum and cutting a chest open will save a patient's life. Oz articulates this viewpoint himself: "Let me explain why surgeons are assholes. Surgery is controlled arrogance. You think you can take a knife to someone's chest and help him. Who thinks that way? Certainly no normal person. You need that confidence, that certainty to do it" ("The Operator"). In other words, Mehmet already rides the line of confidence and arrogance just by the nature of his chosen profession. Surgeons need inflated egos to be good at their job, and Mehmet's Ivy League education certainly doesn't do anything to negate his ego. It must be his ego, then, which rationalizes the acceptability of making false claims to promote weight loss products on his show.

Dr. Oz habitually touts wonder drugs on *The Dr. Oz Show*. Devoid of any certified health benefits, these drugs would be more accurately labeled "1800s Snake Oil." Seriously. "You may think that magic is make-believe," Oz says at the beginning of a typical show, "but this little bean has scientists saying they have found a magic weight-loss cure for every body type. It's green coffee beans, and, when turned into a supplement, this miracle pill can burn fat fast. This is very exciting. And it's breaking news" (Specter, "Columbia"). And it's totally false. While it would be easy to dismiss Oz's fabrications as mere entertainment, there have been serious consequences to Oz's lies. Companies sold tens of millions of dollars worth of the aforementioned supplement after Oz featured the green coffee beans on television. The Federal Trade Commission reached a settlement of nine million dollars and brought charges against the companies for false and deceptive advertising. The "Oz effect" is the phrase that has come to embody this phenomenon. In a video called "Oz's Three Biggest Weight Loss Lies, Debunked," Vox dismantles Oz's most dubious claims. Dr. Oz presents metabolism boosters as the holy grail of weight loss. Some foods, like coffee or chiles, are known to briefly boost metabolism by minuscule amounts. These changes have no effect on weight loss, as they are almost immeasurable and only momentary. Additionally, Oz regularly entices his audience members to "blast away" their belly fat. The notion that weight loss could be targeted towards belly fat is plain rubbish. As previously noted, Oz claims that miracle pills can stimulate weight loss. Oz advocates for these dietary supplements on almost every show. Often these substances prove utterly benign in terms of physiological effect. For this reason, the wholesale fraud characteristic of their marketing amounts to pure thievery ("Dr. Oz's Three Biggest").

Such a degree of blatantly false advertising is concerning in any context. However, as we recall Oz's qualifications as a doctor, his claims become deeply disturbing. He completely forgoes the scientific rigor he demonstrated as a surgical resident at Columbia when he shifts into talk-show host mode. Erin May, a PhD Candidate in Chemical Biology at Harvard University, argues that "Given his education and influence, there's no excuse for the unsubstantiated claims and sensational language that is so pervasive on his show" ("Pulling Back the Curtain"). May goes on to apply the scientific method to some of Oz's dubious claims. One claim she zeroes in on is that garcinia cambogia extract can increase weight loss by 2 to 3 times when compared to diet and exercise alone. May then notes that Oz only alludes to "revolutionary new research," and that his guest can only indicate that the results have been "seen in studies." May makes it clear that neither Dr. Oz nor his guest, Dr. Chen, give "any indication about the size of the study, whether they were placebo-controlled, whether the participants were followed over a long period of time, and [that] there is little mention of safety, or amounts of weight lost." In this scenario, a demonstration involving water being directed from one balloon to another constitutes scientific rigor. Oz's audience ingests this gimmick as veritable proof of the drug's effectiveness, a suitable dumbing down of its biochemical pathway. Oz concludes the segment by showing a 30-second video correlating the drug's effect on the nervous system to beneficial changes in mood and appetite. May highlights the fact that consumers should have major reservations about taking a drug that claims to alter the body's fundamental processes of fat metabolism and neural signaling. Such a drug would be dangerous to take, especially without the oversight of a qualified personal physician. May concludes her analysis by inferring that the drug does not work ("Pulling Back the Curtain").

The uncomfortable truth is that Oz's disregard for the facts must be deliberate. When asked about his relationship with his base of consumers, Oz says "The currency that I deal in is trust, and it is trust that has been given to me by Oprah, and by Columbia University, and by an audience that has watched over six hundred shows" (Specter, "Columbia"). In his mind this trust justifies systematically feeding the public sensationalized misinformation. To Dr. Oz, the support of his fans, Oprah, and Columbia University serves as a license to abandon the scientific method and venture into alternative medicine and pseudo-spiritual healing on his show. The absurdity of these tangents leave the scientifically competent observer almost raw. As Michael Specter puts it, "How are we to react, then, when he offers his show as a platform for Theresa Caputo, a medium who says she can link us with the dead, or Jeffrey Smith, a former yoga instructor whom Oz considers an expert on genetically modified products?" (Specter, "Columbia"). A complete rejection Oz's fantasy world would be a natural reaction at this point.

The evidence against Oz's ethics seemingly demands swift justice.

Before we destroy Oz's last shred of credibility, however, we must consider the possibility that Oz believes these claims to some degree. Oz does have a deeply-held fascination with practices that fall within the scope of eastern spiritual healing. Again, his history explains. As the son of a Turkish immigrant, Oz often made trips to Turkey with his father. In Turkey, he exposed himself to non-Western medical practices. Oz says that in Turkey, "You would never leave a patient in the hospital there unless you had a relative with them. In fact, the nurse gives you the pills to give the patient" (Belluz). Oz argues that while the benefits of practices of this nature may not be verifiable through scientific studies, these customs still hold curative power. Notable is Oz's pre-surgery offering of Reiki treatment to his patients. Reiki, the Japanese practice of laying on one's hands, is derived from the idea that an invisible "life force" flows through the human body. Studies of Reiki routinely show no evidence to support any of its purported positive effects, yet when confronted by a reporter who notes that he is not aware of any evidence-based support for Reiki, Oz quickly responds,

> Neither am I, if you are talking purely about data. But this is one of the fundamental disconnects between Western medicine and what people often refer to as complementary medicine. Not everything adds up. It's about making people more comfortable. I offer things like massage therapy, and offered Reiki if people wanted it. I did not recommend it, but I let people know it was their choice. (Specter, "Columbia")

Oz's fascination with Eastern healing isn't just a personal sidetrack; rather, it's an ingrained mindset, informing medical practice in his workplace at the New York Presbyterian Hospital. Oz's academic peers have different stances on the subject.

These colleagues' perspectives range from passively unconcerned to extremely critical. The most notorious example of criticism comes from a group of scientists, professors, and doctors led by Stanford University's Henry Miller, which wrote a letter calling for Oz's dismissal from the Columbia faculty. "Dr. Oz is guilty of either outrageous conflicts of interest or flawed judgments about what constitutes appropriate medical treatments, or both," the letter claims. It further states, "Members of the public are being misled and endangered, which makes Dr. Oz's presence on the faculty of a prestigious medical institution unacceptable" (Gifford). Alternatively, some members of academia closest to Oz hold decidedly uncritical views on his unorthodox practices. Dr. Michael Argenziano, a colleague of Oz's at Columbia who has known Oz for more than 25 years, reminds us that "When [Oz] was young and just starting out, [he] was practicing what he's now preaching. He was always very committed to preventive medicine, holistic natural health" (Belluz). Even 10 years before Oz went on TV, he studied "alternative medicine, hypnosis, Eastern medicine, all that stuff—guided imagery, acupuncture," according to Argenziano. Another one of Dr. Oz's colleagues, Dr. Richard Green, associate chief of cardiac, thoracic, and vascular surgery at New York-Presbyterian/Columbia University Medical Center, goes a step further by downright praising Dr. Oz. For an interview with *Vox*, Dr. Green said, "He's a brilliant mind," "He's a very charming person," "He has great energy," "He's uniformly respected and admired here," "Maybe he should be president. I would vote for him," "He's a talent. He's multidirectional," and "As for the other doctors who are on TV, I don't put them in [Oz's] league. Not even close." Green even suggests that the leveling off of obesity rates in the US is partially due to Oz's TV influence (Belluz). The staggering diversity of professional opinion on Dr. Oz is difficult to reconcile. It points to the growing disconnect between the perception of reality and factual reality in our nation. The Senate's consumer protection panel acted on behalf of the American public when it attempted to set the record straight in 2014.

Led by Senator Claire McCaskill, the Senate's consumer protection panel questioned Dr. Oz for his complicity in the promotion of dubious weight loss products. After quoting a number of false claims from Oz on his show, Senator McCaskill pointedly asks, "I don't get why you need to say this stuff because you know it's not true." Oz retorts:

I actually do personally believe in the items that I talk about on the show. I passionately study them. I recognize that oftentimes they don't have the scientific muster to pass as fact... My job, I feel, on the show is to be a cheerleader for the audience. And when they don't think they have hope, when they don't think they can make it happen I want to look everywhere, including at alternative healing traditions for any evidence that might be supportive to them. (Wiener-Bronner)

Oz views himself as a cheerleader, who through whatever methods necessary must inspire his audience toward better health. Oz's self-defense is highly indicative of an "end justifies the means" mentality. This philosophy goes hand in hand with Dr. Oz's willingness to circumvent the scientific method. Oz's ascension to cultural stardom formed a citizen of an alternate America in which truth is engineered according to self-preservation.

The upheaval of fact-based reality has created desperate divisions in the United States. Dr. Green exhibits a degree of complicity in the widespread undermining of truth. When asked about Oz's false claims, he responded, "Why would anyone mistake that for anything but entertainment?" (Wiener-Bronner). They don't mistake Dr. Oz for a mere entertainer because Dr. Oz deals in the currency of trust. He wooed his base with his charm and talent, and now they idolize him religiously. His craving for admiration guided his life to its current state. He lives comfortably in a non-factual reality of his own creation, even evading repercussions from the United States Senate. Does this sound familiar? We can no longer claim that earthquake of November 8, 2016 had no warning tremors.

The parallels between Dr. Oz and Donald J. Trump are gravely disturbing. Now, I must note that in all likelihood Dr. Oz has never been called a "fucking moron" by anyone, let alone a Secretary of State. I'm sure Oz would gladly compare IQs with Trump, but if we can set aside the intellectual disparity, both men have led lives of similar trajectories. Both hold MBAs from the Wharton School of the University of Pennsylvania. Each boasts a notable professional career followed by a shift to the entertainment industry, Trump on *The Apprentice* and Oz on *The Dr. Oz Show*. Each crafted his last name into a major brand. "Trump" (ostensibly) means "wealth" while "Oz" (ostensibly) means "health." Oz and Trump wove a perception of themselves as outsider figures to the medical and political establishments, respectively. At their cores, both Trump and Oz derive their self-worth from admiration, each being an excellent entertainer. Devoid of coherent political strategy, a Trump rally amounts to little more than nationalistic showmanship. *The Dr. Oz Show* is more of an outlet for aging women to indulge their fantasy of youthful health than it is programming bearing any semblance to sound medical advice. Unsurprisingly, these men are no strangers to each other.

Trump released his long awaited health records on *The Dr. Oz Show* in early September 2016, capitalizing on the fallout the viral video of Hillary Clinton's near-collapse the week before. Dr. Oz managed to hold Trump's attention for the whole segment, getting him to settle down and stay on topic (a stand-alone, commendable feat of its own). This much-subdued version of Trump was then broadcast to Oz's base of mostly women, making Trump seem like a palatable alternative to Clinton in the final weeks leading up to the election. Oz and Trump effectively portrayed an image of Trump's health, with Trump regularly citing his family history of good genes and Scottish heritage. When the topic of weight came up, Trump capitalized on the moment by conceding that everyone has a little weight to lose and that he's always been "a little bit like this." Compare this to Hillary Clinton's regiment of "yoga, swimming, walking, and weight training" in addition to a diet "rich in lean protein, vegetables, and fruit" and Trump took the win by being more human. CNN summarized the whole charade brilliantly: "Dr. Oz's latest bean is orange and shaped like Donald Trump" (Vox). Overall, Dr. Oz worked his magic in selling the character of Donald Trump as fit for office.

The "Oz effect" may be best understood a microcosm of the present state of American democracy. A precursor to the post-truth era of American politics, *The Dr. Oz Show* reveals the extent to which humanity will forfeit facts for the frenzy of TV spectacle. My diagnosis is this: that Dr. Oz exhibits symptoms of post-truth complicity to a stunning degree. His purported brilliance shreds the possibility that he's hiding behind a feigned stance of ignorance under examination. He created a pathogen bearing his name, a truly horrifying disease and sadly only a foretaste of things to come. My recommended treatment? The American public must follow Toto's lead by peeling back the curtain on engineered, elitist extravaganza.

Works Cited

Belluz, Julia. "The Making of Dr. Oz: How an Award-Winning Doctor Turned Away from Science to Embrace Fame." Vox, 16 Apr. 2015 AAAAAwww.vox.com/2015/4/16/8412427/dr-oz-health-claims.

Gifford, Bill. "Opinion | Dr. Oz Is No Wizard, but No Quack, Either." The New York Times, AAAAA25 Apr. 2015, www.nytimes.com/2015/04/26/opinion/sunday/dr-oz-is-no-wizard-but-no-quack-either.html.

"Pulling Back the Curtain on Dr. Oz." Policylab, AAAAAwww.hcs.harvard.edu/~policylab/2013/06/14/pulling-back-the-curtain-on-dr-oz/.

Specter, Michael. "The Operator." The New Yorker, 19 June 2017, AAAAAwww.newyorker.com/magazine/2013/02/04/the-operator.

---. "Columbia and the Problem of Dr. Oz." The New Yorker, 19 June 2017, AAAAAwww.newyorker.com/news/daily-comment/columbia-and-the-problem-of-dr-oz.

Vox, Ford. "Trump and Oz: A Match Made in Tv Heaven." CNN, Cable News Network, 18 Sept. 2012, www.cnn.com/2016/09/16/opinions/trump-clinton-health-war-vox-opinion/index.html.

voxdotcom. "Dr. Oz's Three Biggest Weight Loss Lies, Debunked." YouTube, 25 Aug. AAAAA2014, www.youtube.com/watch?v=40uh5WGamv4.

Wiener-Bronner, Danielle. "Senators Question Dr. Oz Over Sketchy Diet Solutions." The Atlantic, Atlantic Media Company, 17 June 2014, AAAAAwww.theatlantic.com/national/archive/2014/06/dr-oz-diet-pills-hearing/372964/.

Our Disappearing Shorelines

by Sydnie Boulé
From English 125
Nominated by Catherine Fairfield

Sydnie Boulé's essay "Our Disappearing Shorelines" weaves together the personal, the fictional, and the factual to intervene into critical discussions of climate change. Our English 125 class theme was "Writing the Future." Together we spent the semester exploring the questions of how writing impacts the future and where problem-solving and the literary can meet. One of the themes that we focused on was the role of turning to the past and to memory when writing about the future. Sydnie takes up this question in her poignant reflection on environmental change and how to reconcile the loss of future memories.

Sydnie developed her essay during our class's narrative argument unit. Part of our exploration into writing argumentative papers that utilize creative writing methods was an experiential learning exercise. We took our work outdoors to learn how to write convincingly and persuasively about space and place. Boulé took the seeds of this activity and wrote "Our Disappearing Shorelines." Her narrative goes above and beyond what I thought might come of the exercise, which is a testament to the inspiring creativity that she brought to every one of our class's writing projects.

Catherine Fairfield

Our Disappearing Shorelines

I stood on the deck of the repurposed fishing boat with my daughter Peyton and a dozen or so other tourists as we approached the lighthouse perched on top of its little island. The other passengers who were my age were remarking how incredible the scene was. Not incredible in the sense that there was a lighthouse on an island off the coast—for those of us who had grown up here the Montauk lighthouse was a well-known monument at the very eastern end of Long Island, New York—but incredible for the fact that this lighthouse had once been very much a part of the 120 contiguous miles of Long Island. None of us on that boat could have imagined that in our lifetime the oceans would have swallowed up the Hamptons and the rest of the north and south forks of Long Island, except for a tiny speck of soil supporting the most prominent landmark in the summer playground of the mega-wealthy and those dreaming of one day joining them in their very own mansion on Dune Road. Global warming was now as real as it could possibly be and the consequences were so far beyond what I ever could have imagined that I started to cry as the boat made its way past the lighthouse.

We were warned that this might happen. We were warned that the ocean would invade our beautiful island. Those in the middle of the island felt no need to worry. They believed the water would never reach them. We all believed that the water would never reach us. We lived in our houses and felt, well, untouchable. Long Islanders made it through Hurricane Sandy back in 2012. We suffered for weeks without electricity and poured millions of dollars into rebuilding our beautiful sand beaches and boardwalks. We did not see that as a warning. Maybe we should have paid more attention.

Videos emerged of the hurricane doing damage to our shorelines. The oceans roared with anger, crying out for help. Telling us that we had to stop. We had to change our ways. But after the horrific event, nothing changed. There was no major environmental change made by the government. There were no community plans put into place to decrease our carbon footprint. I remember returning to school after two weeks of isolation. The teachers told us they would be there for us. They said they would be willing to talk with any student about how they felt. Then they said to turn to page six of our textbooks.

People only cared for the moment, and once the moment was over they would go back to their day-to-day lives, the warning of Hurricane Sandy a distant memory.

Twenty-five years later, I cannot say that I did not notice what was happening. Year by year as I brought Peyton to the beach there would be less and less sand. Everyone noticed. How could you not notice? But we all stood silently choosing to enjoy our memories with friends and family at the beach rather than envision a day where we wouldn't have these memories.

I remember my childhood. My parents would take me out to Amagansett each summer for a week of what my mother would call "utter bliss." None of us wondered if there would be a spot on the beach for us to sit and enjoy. The beautiful beaches of the South Shore of Long Island stretched for what seems like an eternity. There were miles of hotels and at the end of the island was Hither Hills State Park where people would set up campsites on the beach. It was a picture perfect summer year after year. It seemed as if our utter bliss would last forever, but slowly we began to see changes. People would have to pay extra to rent a plot on the beach. With the beaches shrinking, there was less room for all of the hotel guests. The prices for camping on Hither Hills skyrocketed to the point where several families could no longer vacation. Restaurants on the water began closing as the insurance prices kept rising. Locals began to move farther west on the island where they did not have to worry as much for the wellbeing of their home. Eventually, my family stopped going out east too. It had gotten to the point where high tide would surpass the dunes and start to flood the lower levels of the hotels. People were scared to go out to utter bliss.

It was a sad ending to witness. Many thought this problem would be resolved, but a lot of us felt that we were in too deep. They had said in news articles that we were beyond the point of return. As a teenager I remember reading an article in *The New York Times* stating that "Rising seas, which already endanger coastal communities through tidal floods and storm surges, could rise three feet or more over the next century if emissions continue at a high level, threatening many shoreline communities" (Schlossberg). This information was public knowledge. It was not as if people did not know that this could very well be our reality in the near future. The article continued to state, "We just don't know how people are going to act" (Schlossberg). The problem was that people did not act. They continued to put these issues in the back of their minds and ignore their neighbors having to evacuate their South Shore homes every time a violent storm blew in. I feel guilty for taking part in not acting, knowing that I could have made even the slightest of a difference.

I think that part of the problem was that many of the articles being written about the effects of climate change were not being focused on where we were living. For example, a 2017 article from *The New York Times* titled "In Peru's Deserts, Melting Glaciers Are a Godsend (Until They're Gone)" reported on how the glacial melt in the Andes has had extreme effects on the environment of Peru and its native people. In the long term, the melting ice caps can harm an entire environment by releasing heavy metals, "leaking into the groundwater supply, turning entire streams red, killing livestock and crops, and making the water undrinkable" (Casey). In the short term, Peru uses the water from the melting ice caps to fuel a hydroelectric plant which "provides power to 50,000 people" (Casey). But without the water from the ice caps, which may not be around in the long run, new methods of farming and generating electricity will need to be created. These complicated trade-offs were taking place in Peru, but again it was in Peru. People would read this article, say "that's awful," and continue on with their day, possibly just reading the next article in the *Times*.

People reading this article who were residents of Long Island did not think of this as a warning sign. I remember a middle-aged man saying "Oh, that's happening in a third world country. Nothing we need to worry about on Long

Island." I wish I would have stood up and said to them, "No, you know this is something you should be worrying about. It is your beaches that will be next. You can kiss your summer weekends in the Atlantic with your children goodbye. You can leave behind late night concerts on the bay at Jones Beach. You can forget about getting a lobster roll at Jordan Lobster Farms with the summer smell of the salty ocean in the background. You can forget about seeing dolphins swimming along the shore early in the morning with the Long Beach surfers. You can never be bothered by a hungry seagull again, and I am sure you may even miss it. You need to stop and think about these things, about the future you are leaving behind for your children and their children. You need to worry!" I wish I had said all of these things. I really did. But instead, I just walked by the man, as it was none of my business to interject my opinion onto an already angry New Yorker. I realize that my timidness contributed to the world my daughter lives in now. I wish that people would have taken the threats more seriously. I wonder if people feel the same as I do. I wonder if they miss it, all the memories they once shared at the beach. Maybe they do, maybe they don't. I sure as hell do.

I look down as Peyton as she takes in the view of the now-isolated mighty Montauk lighthouse. Her eyes are filled with awe as mine are filled with tears. I wish she could have known what it was like to climb to the top of the lighthouse as a child and feel like you were on top of the world. I wish she could have had the struggle of biking 20 miles to the lighthouse with her dad, as I did with mine. I wish I could have taken her on family vacations to Amagansett with everlasting memories of her small feet in the warm sand. I wish she could have experienced the piercing cold water soothing the sunburn on her back and jumping in the waves letting her troubles fade away with each swell. I wish she could have seen what life should have been like for her out east on Long Island. Memories I know I will never forget. Memories Peyton will never have.

I listened to other parents my age tell their children stories about what it was like before the water had taken over. It was sad to see our kids excited, especially knowing that this was something they should not be excited about.

The fact that the tour company made it seem like this was a sight of pure beauty angered me. I looked down at Peyton with her beautiful blue eyes that reflected the glass windows at the top of the lighthouse. I could tell that the wheels in her head were spinning about what the land under here once looked like. I reached down and stroked her hair as it blew in the damp breeze.

"Look, mom!" Peyton yelled out as she pointed to the few inches of sand on the island that remained above water. "I see a shell!"

"It's been awhile since I've seen one of those," I whispered in a soft tone.

"Why don't we collect them, Mom?" she said as she grabbed my hand and stared up at me.

"Yes," I replied, "I think that is a great idea, Peyton."

I snapped a picture of the shell quickly, fearing we might never see one again; this way I knew Peyton would always have something to look at to remember one of the greatest treasures Long Island had to offer.

We watched the lighthouse disappear as the boat started the ten mile trek back to our cars, which were in the nearest available parking lot. The ocean was rough and angry, rocking our boat back and forth. It was as if the ocean was mad at us for creating this world, for expanding it to a size too great for even it to handle. It was our fault, after all, my generation. There was no one else to blame. We watched as a large wave lapped at the base of the lighthouse and I wondered how much higher the water could rise. Was it possible that one day the entire lighthouse would be gone? And the rest of Long Island? Could everyone's favorite place be gone? Simply gone? In the blink of an eye? Completely swallowed by the cold abyss of the never ending rising ocean?

Works Cited

Casey, Nicholas. "In Peru's Deserts, Melting Glaciers Are a Godsend (Until They're Gone)." *The New York Times*, The New York Times Company, 26 Nov. 2017, www.nytimes.com/2017/11/26/world/americas/ peru-cli mate-change.html?rref=collection%2Fsectioncollection%2F climate&action=click&contentCollection=climate&region=stream& module=stream_unit&version=search&contentPlacement= 11&pgtype=sectionfront. Accessed 4 Dec. 2017.

Schlossberg, Tatiana. "Rising Sea Levels May Disrupt Lives of Millions, Study Says." *The New York Times*, The New York Times Company, 14 Mar. 2016, www.nytimes.com/2016/03/15/science/rising-sea-levels-global- warming-climate-change.html. Accessed 4 Dec. 2017.

Matt Kelley/Granader Family Prize for Excellence in First-Year Writing

On behalf of the Sweetland Center for Writing I am pleased to congratulate Rita Hathaway and Ying-Husan Wu, winners of the Granader Family Prize for Outstanding Writing Portfolio; Pok Yu Chan and Dorcas Li, winners the Granader Family Award for Excellence in Multilingual Writing; and Wisteria Deng and Zofia Ferki, winners of the Matt Kelley/ Granader Family Award for Excellence in First-Year Writing. Our judges noted the overall strength of this year's student nominees. Our winners distinguished themselves by presenting finely crafted writing that is engaging and thought provoking.

We also thank instructors for nominating their students and consistently providing high quality writing instruction. I am grateful to my colleagues in the Sweetland Center for Writing who served as judges for this year's writing prizes: Scott Beal, Louis Cicciarelli, Lillian Li, Shuwen Li, Christine Modey, Simone Sessolo, and Naomi Silver. I am especially grateful to Angie Berkley, Jimmy Brancho, Cat Cassel, Raymond McDaniel and Carol Tell, who volunteered to serve as members of the writing prize committee and graciously accepted extra reading and tie-breaking duties. My sincere thanks to Laura Schuyler for guiding the writing prizes cycle from beginning to end, and Aaron Valdez, who creates these beautiful volumes. Finally, I offer my heartfelt thanks to the Granader Family for their generous support of the writing prizes. We hope you enjoy reading these essays as much as we did.

Dana Nichols
Lecturer, Sweetland Center for Writing

Six Reasons

by Wisteria Deng
From RCCORE 100
Nominated by Leslie Stainton

Wisteria Deng is gifted in both poetry and prose, and this essay is eloquent proof. It's a haunting reflection on the author's enduring grief at the loss of her much loved father, a man who hated the smell of mahogany and cherished his only daughter. With its powerful sensory details, beautiful storytelling, and authorial candor and humility, the piece exemplifies the traits of the best essay-writing. It is both lyrical and clear, whimsical and deeply felt, and its portrait of familial love is simply heart-rending.

Leslie Stainton

Six Reasons

Ghosts are real. They don't live in your closet and cause meaningless paranormal activities. Instead, they live in your brain, the deepest layer, the one in charge of faded memories, lost connections and dead selves. Everyone has his own ghost. A ghost that whispers exclusively to the host, days and nights. My ghost is five years and sixty-nine days old now. He has been repeating the same sentence, throughout those five years and sixty-nine days.

"Write it!" He bugs me.

"Write it!"

"Write about your loss (as people euphemize it, avoiding the ugly word "death" as if dodging an infectious disease). Write about the art of losing (how poetic)."

But he is not an art. He is not an object to be discussed. He is, as simple and pure as anything can be, a father – my father.

And I can't write about my father.

I can't write about my father because I am too reluctant to use "was" instead of "is." What fits the grammar does not fit him. He is not a past tense. He is happening, a ghost navigating through my mind. He is now.

I can't write about my father because he is a number, and you don't write about a number. After the big day, his remains were put into a box, sealed, numbered, buried, and vanished. People say that death ends a life. People are wrong. Death doesn't end a life. It changes a life, a vulnerable and transient being, into a serial number tagged on a mahogany urn.

He always hated the smell of mahogany: "The smell of turkey overburnt," so he said. If he had to become a part of nature, instead of the wood, he should belong to the ocean. He is the force of waves crashing on the shore, the overwhelming immensity an ocean embodies, and the promising rhythm of tides dancing with the moon. Every natural element has a nemesis. Wood hates fire. Rain resents the cold. But ocean is different. The ocean embraces everything that comes to her, as did my father. His passion swirls like the ocean. A passion for every little joyous incident in life, for every piece of being that makes up the world. Festivals always gave him the excuse to unleash his fervor. Every lunar new year, he would turn all the lights on at home, clean the house inside-out, open a bottle of wine, and treat me and my mother like two princesses visiting from a foreign land. He would lift up the wine bottle and read the label out loud.

"Chateau De Fouscolombe, 1996. 12.5% vol...75...something..."

Then he would stop reading. He hated the numbers.

"How could you label something so complicated and richly layered?"

Would he know? Less than a year later, he would be numbered and labeled like a bottle of wine.

"How could you label anything?" I murmured, lifting up the urn. "How could you label an ocean?"

I can't write about my father because I am him, and you can't write about yourself. Many people grow up with the saying "don't be like your father." Not me. I grew up becoming more and more similar to my father. Both writers. Weird ones. People who would go crazy over small and nonsensical things. He used to play a poetry writing game with me, in which I had to write two lines about anything he said.

"Two lines about an elephant!"

"But I've never seen an elephant..."

"Doesn't matter. Neither have I. Just write it!"

Then the prompt became an owl, a fire-puffing dragon, a phoenix flying away from the flame...

The writing game continued in his final days. After the stroke that shut down his brain, he lost all of his consciousness, shrinking into a small boy. How close our existence is to its opposite. How perfectly a circle forms as life runs its course. I sat on a chair next to him, the tiny man who was once an owl, a fire puffing dragon, a phoenix flying away from the flame.

"Okay, now let's write about an elephant. Dad, two lines about an elephant!"

I can't write about my father because I have already forgotten about him. After his death, I allocated a specific time period every day to think about him. It started with half an hour, during which I would do nothing other than recollecting every piece of him in my memory, like a little child solving a jigsaw puzzle. But the puzzle was too hard to solve.

I had lost them: the puzzles that gave the shape of a father, my father, piece by piece. I found myself having trouble recalling his voice, his height and even his face. Instead, everything I remembered about him is in tiny fragments. His pitch always went a little higher when he called my name, like a swimmer stretching his body to get ready for a sprint. His lips skewed to the right like the edge of a sword pointing to a side. His eyes: sunshine splinters across the ocean, fireworks to light up the starry night like the fourth of July... But is he still my father? Could the jigsaw pieces ever make up a real man again? In my memories, he becomes a man of perfection, with the right amount of hair covering the right portion of his forehead, just enough to make him look smart but not too much an introvert. His skewed lips form a nice angle that no longer resembles a sharp sword, but a fallen leaf, teasing playfully with the late night air. He becomes a construct of mine. Not real, though real enough for me. More real than the number on a mahogany urn, the "Mr" in a stranger's eulogy, and a stack of faded photos.

I can't write about my father because writing means boundaries, but he is infinity. The fact of his nonexistence gives him the ability to exist ubiquitously. I dreamed of him the night before my first day in college, again when I traveled to the US and started a new life. It seems like my father, the father who once flew five hundred miles just to hear his daughter recite a poem, still refuses to miss out on the important events in my life.

I can't write about my father because I have run out of ways to say "I love you." So I say nothing, instead watch the sunset drift across the ocean, like a fire-puffing dragon, a phoenix flying away from the flame into another space, a space within and beyond him, within and beyond me.

As Time Ticks By

by Zofia Ferki
From RCCORE 100
Nominated by Leslie Stainton

A smart and searingly funny writer, Zofia Ferki tackles a serious topic--Lyme disease, and the tiny tick that infected her with it while she was in high school. Zofia deftly employs a range of creative nonfiction techniques--notably dialogue, telling details, and storytelling--to recount her changing thoughts about the tick as she watches its swollen body gradually deteriorate over the course of 7 weeks while, per doctor's orders, it hangs in a plastic bag on her mother's refrigerator. Zofia cleverly structures the piece chronologically and skillfully weaves in research as she narrates her growing fondness for the insect that has compromised her health. The result is a marvelously charming, yet moving, essay that ends on a surprisingly sobering note.

Leslie Stainton

As Time Ticks By

It is an unspoken rule that the fronts of refrigerators are to be used for scrapbooking. My family was no exception to this rule. I grew up on the face of our fridge. Next to Pablo Picasso's Guernica and the coupons for Papa John's, there I was losing teeth, digging for crabs at the beach, or graduating. The refrigerator was home to season tickets. It was home to Christmas cards from the cousins. And for two months when I was twelve, to a Lyme-disease-carrying deer tick in a Ziploc plastic baggie.

Diagnosis:

"Oh my God."

Something swollen and blue has fallen into the bathroom sink while I am taking off my shirt. It has swirled around in the drain, and now it is struggling to free itself from the pinch of my fingers. I look to my shoulder to find a bruise, equally swollen, bulging from my skin like a fig.

"Oh my God."

"Stop saying that!" my dad calls from the other room.

I point my hickey out to him, along with the thing that kissed me.

"Oh wow… we should probably call the doctor."

One phone call later, and I'm sitting on the counter as my mom paces the kitchen.

"Well, you've got Lyme disease."

"What does that mean?"

"It means you've got bacteria living in your body that shouldn't be there. It means you'll be taking these for a while." She shakes the bottle of Doxycycline capsules from the pharmacist.

"What about the tick?"

"The doctor says we should keep it around in case they need it for medical testing. I've put it in a little bag so it can't get away."

"We can't just kill it?"

"No."

My mom sticks the bagged tick on the refrigerator, where we can keep an eye on it. We hang it from the side of the fridge with a magnet. The magnet has a lady on it who is watering some flowers in her garden. The flowers say, "Bloom where you are planted."

Week 1: The tick is not enjoying bag-life, and I am not enjoying Lyme disease. I cannot see the tick's eyes, but I imagine we're having a staring contest.

"You deserve to live in there you know; it's because of you I don't feel well. I looked you up. You gave me bacteria - they're called Borrelia Burgdorferi. You kept them in your stupid gut, and then you spit them up into my bloodstream. On Google Images, they look like little pasta. I have pasta in my BLOOD. And even worse, I have to take these things for 6 weeks! I wave the orange pill bottle in its face. I hope you die soon."

Week 2: If I tilt the bag slightly, I can peer up at the thing from underneath. From above, it doesn't resemble a tick so much as it does a graying, groping grape. From below, the anatomy becomes more readily visible. At the very forefront of the tick, almost like a beak, projects the tick's gnathosoma, or capitulum. Along the capitulum are the hypostome, where the tick keeps its six rows of tiny teeth, and the chelicerae, which are not visible now, but which were exposed when they were used to cut into my skin. Further down the body is the scutum, the dark cape that covers most of what one might consider to be the head. On either side of this are the eyes (although I can't see them from this angle), and below the scutum on the front are the fovea. The fovea are dots and there are two of them. The legs are disgusting and there are six of them. Of course, I won't know any of this until years later. All I know now is that my stomach hurts and I should probably go throw up soon.

Week 3: I throw open the kitchen door.

"GUESS WHAT I FOUND OUT TODAY, I scream at the tick. "This, this... THING you gave me - IT'S PERMANENT!" I dash over to the sink to vomit. "Your little pasta friends make me feel like CRAP. I barely even go to school anymore. The only food that doesn't make me feel queasy is YOGURT. I have to sleep with a trashcan next to my bed, and when I wake up I can't even move because your germs take over my muscles and make them stiff. And Mom says there are going to be traces of these spirochetes inside of me forever! I'm so sick of seeing you here every morning, sitting among the family photos as if you own the place. I wish we could just throw you out already. I know the doctor says we're supposed to keep you around, but if it were up to me you'd be in a dump somewhere. It's what you deserve."

I turn to the tick which has turned into a balloon and is passed out in the corner of the bag.

"Oh, I forgot. You don't even care because you're just fat and happy after feeding on my blood."

I think the tick is mocking me. It's actually just molting.

Week 4: At first, I think the tick has died. I see its empty carcass lying broken and empty along the bottom of the bag. I bend down to get a closer look. Then I realize it's just a shell.

"AAAH."

The tick is peering at me from above. It is enormous now, and its sudden increase in size has startled me. It is hanging from the blue Ziploc lining at the top of the bag, grasping at the plastic with its new pair of grappling-hook legs. Looking at the newly emerged nymph, I am reminded of Mothra and the sci-fi movies I used to watch with my dad.

A shadow falls over the city of Charlottesville. It's a bird... It's a plane... It's Tickzilla! Citizens pour out of buildings and into the streets to gape in awe at this monstrosity. Its legs, the size of skyscrapers. Its chelicerae, the size of trains - it uses them all to wreak havoc on the townspeople. Run or hide if you'd like, but there's no escaping Tickzilla....

"Ever consider using your powers for good and not for evil?" I watch the tick romping around its enclosure, laughing to myself. "You probably think you're so cool."

When the sun shines in through the kitchen window, it glints off the tick's body armor and suddenly I am staring at a robot from the distant future. When the sun fades, the tick crouches down into the corner of the bag and is transformed into a ninja, hiding in the shadows. "And sometimes I can't help but agree."

Week 5: "Good morning," I mentally greet the tick as I prepare my breakfast. I've made it to school every day this week, and I'm feeling a bit ambitious. "I could go for some pancakes. Ever had a pancake before?" I look over to the fridge. "Ooh, you're not looking too hot."

The tick is lying crumpled, clutching at itself. Formerly a grape, it is now but a currant, and it is almost difficult for me to differentiate the living body from the molted exoskeleton. Tickzilla no longer.

"Hey guess what." I reach on top of the fridge and snatch my pills. "The bottle's almost empty. That means I'm nearly done!"
I peer through the orange plastic of the pill container and the fridge surface is immediately painted yellow. I am greeted by dozens of smiles, which wink up at me from the multitude of photographs. Even the lady's flowers are grinning as she waters them. Trapped in its bag, the tick doesn't seem to care.

"That's okay. I didn't expect you to understand."

As I rummage around the pantry for the pancake mix, it occurs to me that the tick hasn't eaten for a long time. It's probably going to die soon. I almost feel a bit bad.

Week 6: It's Sunday, and I've pulled a stool over to the fridge so I can sit and examine the tick for a while. It's exhibited almost no movement over the past few days, and it's clear that there isn't much time left for the family arachnid. I let out a sigh that rustles the bag.

"You know, I've been thinking. You probably don't do much thinking. Your brain is probably like a grain of sand. You probably just eat and sleep and, well…." I scan the bottom of the bag for fecal matter. "Well anyway, I doubt you're capable of real thought. I doubt you even know I'm here right now. You're just a parasite and you probably don't even know it. You were made to suck other people's blood. That's something you have to do, just like this Doxycycline is something I have to take until this bacteria you gave me is mostly gone. You're stuck to eating from hosts like me just like I'm obliged to making sure you never infect anyone again. Your bag, my disease, it's a life of confinement for you and me. I reach out with a finger and touch the tick through the plastic. I guess we're confined to a lot of things…."

Week 7: I wake up one morning to find that the tick is dead. She is curled up in fetal position, legs in the air, next to her other carcass. Two empty bodies. Aside from me and my deceased tick, The kitchen is alive with the clatter of breakfast preparations. My family fails to realize they are standing in a morgue. I am tempted to shush them out of respect for the dead. Instead, I just stand there staring at the fridge.

"Hey Zof, we don't need that tick anymore." My mom leans against the counter, crunching on an English muffin. "You can throw that nasty bag away now."

"I know…."

"It's gonna be so nice not having to look at that thing anymore. Yuck. What a horrid little creature."

"Yeah I guess…."

It takes me a few days to summon the courage to remove my tick from her spot on the fridge. Eventually, I open the cupboard to the trashcan and toss in the baggie as well as the pill bottle - also empty. I picture the tick lying in a dump somewhere. In a way, I realize I am finally setting her free.

"Goodbye," I whisper.

The only vestiges of our parting are to be found squirming around in the tissues of my body. I will never be saying goodbye to them.

Endnotes

1   **One phone call later:** It may strike the reader as odd here that I never actually visited the doctor. Apparently, my rash at the site of the bite was so characteristic of Lyme disease that the doctor felt comfortable diagnosing me over the phone. The over-the-phone diagnosis was also the reason why the doctor wanted to keep the tick around just in case it needed to be medically tested - because I never was!

3   **"IT'S PERMANENT":** It turns out that there is actually controversy in terms of how "permanent" Lyme disease actually is. According to the CDC, though certain effects of Lyme disease (such as long-term nerve damage) may be permanent, if a patient is diagnosed quickly enough, the Lyme disease itself may be cured with antibiotic treatment. However, according to the Bay Area Lyme Foundation, tests have revealed that *Borrelia burgdorferi* have been "found in many tissues and organs including the skin, joints, heart, brain, bladder and other sites of untreated animals as well as in animals who receive antibiotic treatment." This is evidence that Lyme disease may not be entirely curable, even with antibiotic treatment.

6   *I doubt you even know I'm here right now:* Apparently, some ticks actually have the ability to detect the presence of hosts based on their carbon dioxide outputs. So it is probable that the tick actually *did* know I was there right then.

6   **The only vestiges:** Again, this passage is based on information provided by the Bay Area Lyme Foundation, which asserts that Lyme disease bacteria continue to reside in the host even after antibiotic treatment.

Bibliography

"Borrelia Burgdorferi." *Bay Area Lyme Foundation*. Bay Area Lyme Foundation, 2017. Web. 16 Apr. 2017.

Fox, Richard. "Invertebrate Anatomy OnLine." *Untitled 1*. Lander University, 29 May 2007. Web. 16 Apr. 2017.

Goltz, Lauren. "Ecology and Disease Potential of the Black-legged Deer Tick, Ixodes Scapularis Say, in Mississippi." *ProQuest*. N.p., 2012. Web. 16 Apr. 2017.

"Lyme Disease." *Centers for Disease Control and Prevention*. Centers for Disease Control and Prevention, 08 Feb. 2017. Web. 16 Apr. 2017.

Vredevoe, Larisa, Ph.D. "Tick Biology." *UC Davis Department of Entomology and Nematology*. University of California, Davis, 2017. Web. 16 Apr. 2017.

Granader Family Prize for Excellence in Multilingual Writing

Comparative Analysis of Two Culturally Distinct Texts: Snickers Got You Snickering

by Pok Yu Chan
From Writing 120
Nominated by Scott Beal

Pok Yu (Wilson) Chan's essay focuses on how Snickers has customized its Hong Kong advertising campaign to appeal to local aesthetics and values. His essay uses comparative analysis to make a purposeful and compelling argument about the specific effectiveness of such "glocalization" for the contemporary Hong Kong market. By situating his analysis within the specific aesthetic and political context of Hong Kong following the umbrella revolution, Wilson gives his argument clear and powerful stakes.

Scott Beal

Comparative Analysis of Two Culturally Distinct Texts:
Snickers Got You Snickering

Snickers chocolate bar, one of the most beloved confectioneries in the US, is also rapidly rising in the global market. Although it is a brand with more than 80 years of history, Snickers is often remembered as a humorous and energetic brand since the launch of the "You are not you when you're hungry" campaign in 2011. With a global sale of $3.572 billion, Snickers led the candy market in 2012 (Schultz). The key to its success is not only the quality and reputation of the product, but also the adaptation of the advertising campaign to the local cultures around the world, or "glocalization" — the hybrid of "globalization" and "localization" in today's market.

These two series of billboard advertisements, one from Hong Kong and the other from the US, both feature quotes in the pieces. The US version, targeting the domestic market, features incorrect quotes from public figures and classic blockbusters that are deliberately edited to be humorous. For example, in one of the pieces, the quote says "You jump, you jump.", which is derived from the famous line "You jump, I jump." in the classic movie *Titanic*. By changing only one single word from the original line, this new quote tells a completely different story by telling viewers that: if Jack was hungry when he was saying the sentence, he would have said "You jump, you jump" instead, which would possibly turn this tragic romance into a comedy. The other quotes from the series are also famous lines that are presumably known by almost everyone in the States, and when it turns up to be different than what people would expect because of the

Original line from the movie *Titanic*: "You jump, I jump."

edition, the whole piece creates a situational ironic effect that makes people laugh. The intention of the advertisement is to vividly demonstrate what these famous quotes might have turned out if the people were hungry when saying them. With the picture of a Snickers chocolate bar and the slogan "You are not you when you're hungry" that is used throughout the entire series, the message of how Snickers can help you quickly fight hunger is immediately clear to viewers.

It is also noteworthy that the background of the print advertisements is not plain solid brown. Instead, a tint of white in the center of the pieces fades in the background in a circle, creating an effect that grasp viewers' attention like shedding a spotlight on the position. The use of the gradual change of the background color as opposed to a simple, monochromatic color does not only make the advertisement more interesting visually, but also reinforces the position of the piece's center of attention. The "spotlight" is put on the quotes instead of the image of the Snickers bar at the bottom of the piece because as an established and popular brand in the US, the name can be easily recognized from afar just for its signature block letters "SNICKERS" in red and blue, making it unnecessary to draw more attention to it. However, as the quotes are the main part of the campaign, and its indirect approach to convey the message of fighting hunger with the humorous revision of the famous quotes requires more thinking for viewers to understand. Therefore the fade in of the white color effectively catches and makes people's attention to stay on the quote until they get the joke.

In comparison, the use of the same "spotlight" effect is found at a different position in the Hong Kong versions. Instead of right in the center of the piece, the tint of white is put behind the image of a Snicker bar and the slogans at the bottom right corner. It is supposed that this adjustment is made because of the assumption that Snickers is less well-known in Hong Kong than US, so that after getting the audience's attention with the amusing slip-ups, the spotlight guides their attention back to the brand itself to strengthen the image of it. This is an essential modification because with all the competition of local and other Asian brands of snacks, Snickers needs people to remember and accept it. The slogan used in the Hong Kong advertisements is also not the direct translation of the one used in the US campaign. Instead, a Chinese eight-word slogan that literally translates to "Doing nine things out of ten wrong - Because you're hungry?" is put under the image of the Snicker bar. This Chinese slogan is not only more interesting but it also rhymes in Cantonese Chinese, making it more catchy and easy to remember for Hong Kong people, who are native speakers of this language.

By making only the necessary changes including changing the position of the spotlight and the slogans, Snickers maintains the iconicity of its image by maximizing the graphical resemblance between the two campaigns. The well-chosen amendments adequately adapt the original for the Hong Kong market, without risking the brand's recognizability or identity. However, the campaign takes a more progressive manner in terms of modifying the texts for this overseas market. Instead of the amended lines from famous movies or people, the Hong Kong version of the campaign features the direct quotes of some slip-ups made by local celebrities or politicians. Many of these slip-ups were made in rather serious settings, including when a lawmaking councilor was being interviewed by journalists, and a meeting in the Legislative Council. Because these errors are so silly, they soon went viral on different social media in Hong Kong, and most of them were even made into memes and ridiculed by netizens for quite an amount of time. That's why the quotes are recognizable even without being marked with references. These hilarious quotes are so familiar to many Hongkongers, especially the younger ones, that they would be able to immediately associate the sentences with the original speakers.

The use of these quotes is smart in two ways. Firstly, it echoes the distinctive "topical sarcasm" culture, or in Cantonese, "cau^1 $seoi^2$". This culture emerged in Hong Kong since the prevalence of online blogging and social media. A work or practice of topical sarcasm chiefly includes addressing or commenting on an issue or person by obliquely referring to another current political issue or famous quote in a sarcastic way, and it is a common manner adopted by many netizens and young people in Hong Kong because they usually don't want to directly offend anyone. Often categorized as a form of derivative work, people who employ topical sarcasm to their creative work sometimes get into disputes over copyrights. Sometimes they are also portrayed as childish, frivolous and unpresentable because of the "jokes" they make. Nonetheless, topical sarcasm has become one of the most predominant internet cultures in Hong Kong, as it is otherwise praised by young people for the witticism and political sensitivity it carries. These advertisements, found in light boxes in subway stations and bus stops, appear to be comical by shattering our expectation of what a conventional advertisement is like.

The use of topical sarcasm is clearly seen in the advertisements. One of the texts from the series is a quote from Henry Tang Ying-yen, who was a politician and one of the candidates of the 2012 Hong Kong Chief Executive (head of the government) election. In an interview, he said, "Protecting [Hong Kong's]

core value, is the core part of the core value." This incomprehensible yet laughable remark he made confused and amused the many in Hong Kong. Ever since, these words have become one of the most iconic things people remember about this ex-candidate.

Text reads: "Protecting the core value, is the core part of the core value."

And sometimes when someone says something that doesn't make sense, people would mock the person by saying something along the lines of " You're talking about Hong Kong's core value now?" or " Why are you trying to be Henry Tang?", even though he has been fairly inactive in Hong Kong's politics and after losing the election in 2012.

Another reason why the use of the quotes is very effective is that it appeals to the people in Hong Kong by recognizing its local culture. Although to a non-Chinese speaker the characters in the advertisement might appear to be no different than any other Chinese words, these texts are actually written in spoken Cantonese Chinese instead of standard written Chinese, which is primarily based on Mandarin Chinese. It is comparable to spelling "though" as the colloquial variant "doe". The use of spoken Cantonese Chinese that is usually only seen on the internet or in other informal occasions has a vital effect on appealing to

Hong Kong people because it sounds more down-to-earth and local. This strategy secures the effective communication of the campaign's message by closing the gap and the sense of distance Hong Kong people might have for this foreign brand.

Additionally, these hilarious quotes are totally local to Hong Kong, including quotes from illogical things politicians have said and anachronic lines from TV drama. When looking at both the Hong Kong and US versions, it is convenient to think that there is nothing special about the both versions of the campaign referring to their own local cultures that are

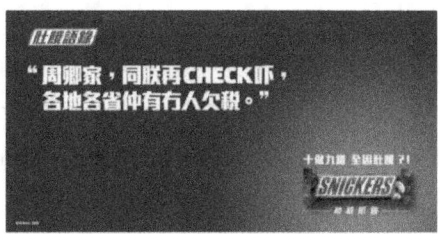

Text reads: "Minister Chow, please 'CHECK' [sic] for me whether there are other people that have been owing taxes ."
(The line comes from a period TV drama set in the Imperial Chinese Ming Dynasty, so the character shouldn't know how to speak English.)

targeted. However, it is important to note that the US is one of the biggest cultural exporters while Hong Kong has relatively limited cultural influence on a global scale. Ranked the 3rd best country in terms of cultural influence ("Cultural Influence Rankings"), the US has been exporting its values, beliefs and lifestyle through mass media, including television, film and music. It imports much less than it exports because many foreign movies find it difficult to have good box offices in the US (Moldagulova). However, Hong Kong is rather welcoming when it comes to foreign entertainment culture. From Hollywood to Bollywood, from US pop to K-pop music, there is usually a market in Hong Kong. And many of the references used in the US advertisements like the movies *Titanic* and *Star Wars* are also well known to many Hongkongers. Therefore, the purpose of using a local Hong Kong reference in the Hong

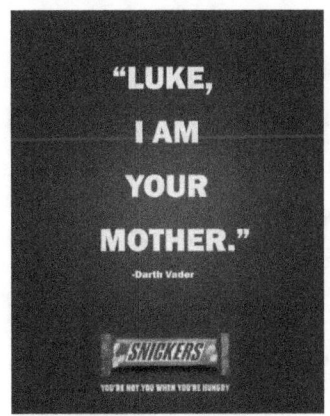

Original line from the movie Star Wars: Episode V: "No, I am your father." But the misquotation "Luke, I am your father." from which the above piece is derived, has been somehow accepted by the general public and popularized.

Kong version in this campaign shall not simply be considered the same as the purpose of using American cultural reference in the original US version. While the use of quotes from American movies and public figures in the US campaign is due to American people's rather limited knowledge and interest of foreign or international affairs and entertainment culture, the use of these local Hong Kong quotes that supposedly only Hong Kong people will pick up is the evidence of the Snickers' appreciation of the local Hong Kong culture, because the corporation could have simply translated the quotes into Chinese, which is also reasonably well-known and understandable to Hong Kong people.

The quotes, or the entire campaign itself, manifest not only cultural but also political significance. As topical sarcasm is the fundamental element of this advertising campaign, its release in 2015 reminded the people in Hong Kong of not only the interviews where the politicians made the silly mistakes, but also other controversial issues and political events that were being discussed around that time. One of the issues is the government's campaign launched in 2008 that has been promoting teaching the Chinese subject using Mandarin instead of Cantonese in elementary and secondary schools, which was widely understood as the government's attempt to assimilate Hong Kong's culture by many people, especially localists. That's why when Snickers, an American brand, is showing recognition of the Cantonese Language and Hong Kong culture, people feel that they are having approval and support from outside. Other than that, the campaign was launched half a year after the end of the Umbrella Movement, where thousands of Hong Kong people went to the streets and stand up for democracy in 2014, this distinctively local voice in the advertisements also appeared to be a subtle support for localism, which is an ideal for many political activists that believe that only through democracy can Hong Kong preserve its core values and unique culture. Especially for the text mentioned in the previous paragraph, where a quote about Hong Kong's core value is featured, it reminds some people of not only the preposterousness of Henry Tang's words, but also the actual core values of Hong Kong, which include the rule of law, human rights, freedom and democracy— what they have been fighting for.

Not surprisingly, many people in Hong Kong loved the advertisements, for its humor, recognition of local culture or the approving response to the localist voices. They went viral on the internet just like the slip-ups once did. Netizens even developed templates so that people can put in quotes or sentences that they found funny and create their own "Snickers hunger quotes". Came as a surprise, this offline-to-online marketing (Chan) works like a tangible interaction between the brand and these potential customers, and also prolonged the fad and heated discussion for quite a while. This is a proof of the successful infusion of local sarcasm to an international brandname that made the local audience enthusiastically embrace the creativity and humor of the foreign corporation.

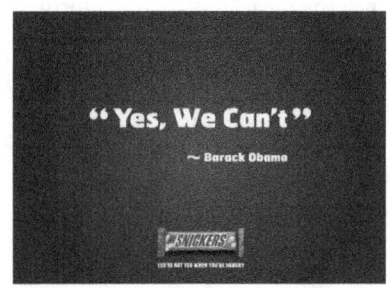

Original slogan from Obama's campaign: "Yes, We Can."

Humor is often incorporated in advertising campaigns. Both advertising campaigns utilized humor to appeal to the audience by making hilarious references to famous quotes from entertainment media and public figures, and of course, successfully captured the public's interest and reinforced Snickers' energetic and lighthearted image. The US campaign realizes the predominance of the domestic entertainment culture in the country, and by re-mentioning some classic lines from classic movies and beloved personalities, including the former president Obama, it guarantees a big audience formed by the preestablished fans and supporters for these movies or people. And the interesting amendment strongly catches people's attention.

Receiving positive responses from the public in US, Snickers, however, did not copy and paste the campaign for the Hong Kong market. It decided to make a witty response to issues that people in Hong Kong are currently concerned with, as well as to glocalize its marketing strategy and campaign to concentrate its effect to Hong Kong. By demonstrating recognition of the local culture in

Hong Kong, Snickers minimizes the effect of cultural homogeneity that is often associated with international corporations. As an international brand, Snickers does not seek to wipe out other local brands or monopolize the market, but to fit into the local Hong Kong culture. By precisely responding to peoples' interest and needs, as well as making people snicker at its advertisements, Snickers has made some smart moves to make both people from the US and Hong Kong to welcome its chocolate bars, and demonstrate the magnitude of glocalization in this more than ever globalized world.

Works Cited

Bennet, Devlin. "| Snickers Advertisement Case Study |" *Blogspot*, 13 Sep 2016, http://devlinbennettgcsemedia.blogspot.com/2016/09/snickers-advertisement-case-study.html. Accessed 7 Nov 2017.

Chan, Jennifer. "Snickers explains its boldest ad ever" *Marketing*, 3 Jun 2015, http:// www.marketing-interactive.com/ snickers-marketing-team-explains-its-boldest-ad-ever/. Accessed 7 Nov 2017.

"Cultural Influence Rankings" US News, https://www.usnews.com/news/best-countries/influence- full-list. Accessed 7 Nov 2017.

Hung, Toby. "'Try my breast': New Snickers ads poke fun at famous slips of the tongue" *Coconuts Hong Kong*, 10 Jun 2015, https://coconuts.co/ hongkong/news/try-my-breast-new-snickers-ads-poke-fun-famous-slips-tongue/. Accessed 6 Nov 2017.

Moldagulova, Zhanna. "Foreign movies can't make it to the U.S." *The Daily Universe*, 16 Apr 2013, http://universe.byu.edu/2013/04/16/foreign-movies-cant-make-it-to-the-u-s1/. Accessed 7 Nov 2017.

Schultz, E.J.. "Snickers Surging To Top Of Global Candy Race" *Ad Age*, 20 Sep 2012, http:// adage.com/article/news/snickers-surging-top-global-candy-race/237349/. Accessed 6 Nov 2017.

Hey, Where are You?

by Dorcas Li
From Writing 120
Nominated by Scott Beal

Dorcas's observations in this essay are so sharp and careful, and each new detail leads us to a new layer of meaning. While there is no straightforward message revealed by the photogravure she analyzes, Dorcas's exploration reveals a nuanced portrait of its sense of loss and disorientation, and of the ambiguous story of the missing girl implied by the juxtaposed images. She has seen into this work deeply, and it's a pleasure to follow along with her attempts to make sense of it.

Scott Beal

Hey, Where are You?

An artwork by Lorna Simpson caught my eyes at the first glance: It is an untitled photogravure of two juxtaposed images with hand-added water color and screen-printed lettering at the bottom. The black-and-white fragment of a piano in the left image reminded me of the past days when I was practicing old melodies on the aged piano with my gray-haired grandma—I squinted my eyes and saw golden specks of dust basking and dancing in the sun ray. In the image at the right, a pair of high heel shoes is sitting quietly on the ground, which seems to indicate that the scenes presented are related to a girl. But, hey, where are you?

There is no sunshine here. The simplicity and the overall dim color of the images struck me hard and gave me a strong sense of loneliness and emptiness; the sentence at the bottom—"What should fit here is an oblique story about absence, but I can't remember the short version"—pulled me even deeper into the abyss of desperation as the seemingly most straightforward clue again contributed to the mystery. Though I couldn't make sense of the images and the caption, I felt the sense of loss. "Is it only the girl that is missing? Is there anything else?" I asked, but there was only silence. "But I can't remember the short version."—Even the memory is lost. Hey, where are you? I dropped down my heavy backpack and sat down against the wall.

The picture made me feel uneasy because I am afraid of the feeling of loss, especially the loss of memory, which creates a huge hole in my heart. My grandpa has Alzheimer's disease, a monster slowly devouring all his precious memories. In the past 10 years, he has gradually forgotten many precious memories; he can no longer recognize me, his most beloved granddaughter. How sad it is when the one who had given you your name and nurtured you with all the love is now saying "I don't know who you are, but I know I love you." Despite not having my heavy backpack sitting on my shoulder, my heart was still heavy.

As I escaped from the mournful memory and went back to the picture, I was still haunted by a gloomy mist of fear and was hesitated to look into the black parts as if they were black holes that would suck me in, and as if they were the Alzheimer's that has erased everything which was supposed to be where the darkness resides. Nevertheless, I felt an internal urge to dig into the story—I wanted to find the lost memory, just as I will always try to help my grandpa pick up all the past stories even if they will soon be lost again.

I took a deep breath and gave a closer look at the picture, hoping to find more clues about the emptiness and the missing parts. The left-side image of the photogravure is totally in grayscale with a part of an upright piano shown in the approximately upper half. It is not a typical depiction of a piano—the black and white alternating keys—but, instead, it is the bottom panel and the pedals that are shown. The first eccentric thing that I noticed at once was the pedals of the piano: it has only two pedals instead of three, as in my memory every piano I have seen has three pedals. For an upright piano, the missing middle pedal is usually a practice pedal with locking option which helps to significantly lower the volume of the sound so that the piano player can practice quietly without disturbing the others. Why is it missing? I thought. Without the practicing pedal, there's no way to conceal the music played. The bottom panel is made of wood with vertical stripes. It is dotted with white spots and scratches near the bottom, which disturb the elegant stripes of the wood, showing that the piano might have a long history.

The whole scene of the image on the left made me feel insecure and unstable—the ground is missing, which is being replaced by a wedge of dimensionless darkness. I guess the lack of dimension and depth of the black area, which occupies the lower half of the image, is the reason why I have the sense of insecurity and fear—I have no idea what's in the darkness. How deep is it? Where does it lead to? I felt like if I don't hold on to the two strangely lonely pedals tightly, I would fall into the endless darkness. The piano might also suddenly fall into the black whole as everything else presumably did. Taking the darkness into account, the image looks ironically discordant: The lower part of the image is pure black, which is darker than the gray panel of the piano. As darker colors are generally perceived as heavier than the lighter ones, the picture is supposed to look stable with the black color lump at the bottom. However, while a piano is usually considered as a bulky and heavy instrument, the black area represents emptiness which doesn't have any weight to it. Thus, it feels strangely unbalanced since the heavy piano is floating on top of emptiness.

My sights drifted to the right side of the picture, where there is finally some color, but desperation remains. There is pair of high heel shoes, the only entity in the whole artwork that seems to be related to the life of the character. The shoes are in khaki suede with old-fashioned spool heels and seem to have been worn for long since the suede looks messy without the uniformed gloss; the color of the shoes looks very dim as if they were covered by a thick layer of dust. However, oddly, the orientation of the shoes is exactly in the direction of how people will normally stand. The two shoes have a short distance between them; the tips of the shoes are pointing to the same direction, but not exactly parallel: they are rotated slightly outward, resembling the natural standing posture of human feet. If I cover up the top part of the picture and only leave the bottom part of the shoes, I would think that there must be someone standing, maybe a transparent girl. Haunted by the infinite darkness, she was so intimidated to even slightly move her feet. She didn't know where to go, her heart was filled with fear, and the darkness silently engulfed her. But I cannot see her, only a silent whisper in my intuition was telling me she might be there. Hey, where are you? There was no answer but only darkness as if the girl who was wearing the high heels just faded, vanished, and blended into the darkness.

The pair of high heels is stepping on a piece of wrinkled dark clothes with a cut nap where scattered gleam falls on. The texture of the clothes indicates that it is most likely pleuche, the most common textile for a piano cover. This was such an interesting realization that evoked many thoughts: Why a pair of high heels is stepping on the piano cover? Where is the piano cover put? An inexplicable fear crept into my heart again, as my view followed the pleuche cloth which quietly sprawled into the depth of the space and disappeared in the darkness. Darkness, again. On this side of the image, it governs almost the upper 80% of the whole space. This time instead of feeling lightweight because of its emptiness, the darkness seems so overwhelmingly condensed and heavy that no oxygen could even squeeze in. I feel like the high heels, instead of bearing the weight of a person, most likely a girl, is bearing the weight of all the darkness. Perhaps that is the reason why the high heels have to be in stool heels, which could give them a bit more strength to stand firm against the weight. There is a ray of light coming from the left side of the picture, illuminating the pleuche and the shoes and casting two shadows beside them. However, even the only ray of light which gave me hope flinched when it encounters the overwhelming dark—the pleuche disappeared into darkness by the tips of the high heel, and the two small shadows sneak into the dark background quietly.

The seemingly isolated images are actually closely related to each other and are jointly telling the story. Aesthetically, the two images have beautiful symmetry—two pedals on the left side, and two shoes on the right. They are both in pairs; however, they happen to convey the same feeling of loneliness: the middle pedal is missing, and the girl who is supposed to be wearing the shoes is missing. Taking a closer look, I realized that the tips of the pedals are glossy, comparing to the rest part, which is most likely due to constant polishing by some smooth surface: either by bare feet or the fabric of socks. The girl who plays the piano may have the habit of taking off the shoes. The high heels at the right side also reflected this possibility since I know it is very hard to press the piano pedal wearing high heels, so the girl probably would want to take them off.

Most importantly, the darkness, the huge chunk that occupies at least half of either of the images, creates the overall desolate and wistful atmosphere, and it was the darkness and emptiness that had triggered lots of my thoughts and rendered me with endless speculation and uncanny fear. Besides the abstract feeling, the darkness somehow points to an alternative of the spatial relationship of the two pictures: the darkness, with the same hue, seems to be connected to each other. Instead of having the two pictures placed side by side, what if we put the left-hand-side picture on top of the right and let the darkness be connected? The two separate fragments of image now become one, and it was quite scary to imagine how the story would be in this case: It seems that except for the piano, everything else in the space has fallen in to the fathomless abyss, and the pair of high heels has fallen onto the ground after a long lonely travel free falling in the dark. However, then, how come the shoes can land so perfectly upright pointing to the same direction? Another one of the essential elements in this picture—the pleuche clothes—indicates the opposite arrangement of the two pictures. If the piece of pleuche cloth is indeed the piano cover and is covering the piano, then the picture on the right is actually somewhere on top of the picture on the left. But there are also unsolved problems: why would somebody put a pair of shoes on top of the piano? Besides, if someone just put the pair of high heels there, the two shoes are most likely to be very close to each since the most convenient way to carry a pair of high heels is to grab both shoes at their counter by one hand and put them down directly. However, the two shoes are standing there apart, as if someone was wearing it. But why would someone stand on top of a piano and just leave with the shoes in place?

After sitting there for two hours staring at the picture and contemplating, still, I couldn't make sense of the story. I was obsessed with all the possibilities and confused by all the seemingly contradictory clues. But one thing that is clear is the sense of loss. It is because of the brokenness of the fragments presented that makes the story obscure and incomplete, and it is because of the darkness of the space depicted that makes the atmosphere pensive and melancholy. I was eager to look at the picture again and again, almost even immerse myself into it. I wanted to shout to the darkness "hey, where are you?" I wanted to bring a torch with me, to expel the darkness and see everything clearly. But I couldn't. There was no more clue to give me a fuller understanding of the whole story. Imagine seeing a scene which indicates that something had just happened some time ago—could be right before you come, could be hours or days ago, or could be weeks or month earlier. You cannot tell exactly when or how that happened, but the things that remain are giving you intriguing but puzzling clues while the character is no longer there. In this situation, I would be really curious and eager to know what the story was and where the people are now. I would regret not being able to arrive a bit earlier. If I come a bit earlier, would I have witnessed or even be a part of the story? All the breathless things are still there—the piano, the plauche cloth, and the pair of high heels—while all the living things are missing—the girl, the story, and the memory. Hey, where are you? I realized that the thing that I cared about was the character, who is alive, who possesses a distinct characteristic, who has secrets and grieves, who has her own story to tell, and who is longing and deserved to be heard.

Time elapsed without disturbing me and people came and went; I was still sitting there. Filled with all the thoughts, I was expecting to find someone who was also interested in this photogravure to talk to. However, another picture next to it, in which figures are wearing clothes with little coverage with their faces covered by single-color paintings, seemed to be more appealing to most people. Two college girls came, one of them stood in front of the piano and high heel picture for a minute and walked away to the next picture as her friend called her. A pair of middle-aged couples came, passed through my picture, and walked up to the next one. I was somehow disappointed. Why wouldn't anybody care about this picture? At last, a young couple brought their daughter. The little girl seemed to be attracted by the piano & high heel picture. She walked to it and called her parents to come. But to my disappointment, her parents, seemed to be in a hurry, just brought her away. It is such an intriguing picture, but why does nobody seem to care? Isn't the absence of all the missing things worth pondering? Isn't the sense of loss an invitation of more care and attention? They might have seen it just as a random capture of some common things, or they may think that the story is too hard to make sense of and they have no time and attention for it.

I somehow feel the same way when I first saw the picture: it looked simple and abstract; it evoked lots of questions, but at the same time its ambiguity seemed to be pushing people away. I guess most of the people were attracted at first but knowing that they cannot get a short and quick grasp of its meaning, they turned around and walked away. I almost had done that when I first saw it. However, as I looked closer, sat down, and spent time with it, there were just more and more thoughts flooding into my mind which I've never expected at the beginning. It was only when I started to care about the underlying story, related the pictures to my own experience, and tried to understand it with love and compassion, could I be able to get connected to it. I have evaluated all possible versions of this story; even though none of them worked perfectly, I realized that it was the compassion, care, and attention to the character that was driving me to dig into it, and to be eager to listen to what the picture has to say.

I ended up not talking to anyone who had passed by that afternoon. I could have stopped one or two of them and started the conversation, but I guessed what should fit here is a short conversation about "Hey, what do you think of this photogravure?" or "What do you think it means?", but I really didn't have a short answer to it—all I have is the long version of my thoughts, imaginations, and feelings, which were so substantial and real, which I couldn't and didn't want to summarize into a short version for people who did not care. There are so many things missing in this picture—not only the girl, not only the middle pedal, and not only the ground—the things truly missing are people's understanding, attention, and care for it.

While I was sitting against the wall, watching people passing by, and having the long version of my stories and emotions in my mind without anybody to share, the girl was sitting in the darkness of the photogravure saying, "What should fit here is an oblique story about absence, but I can't remember the short version". She, too, was waiting for someone who cares to share about her deepest thoughts and feelings, which could never be explained in a short version. Even though I didn't know what exactly she was experiencing, I could feel exactly what she was feeling in the darkness.

Hey, I am here. How are you? I want to listen to your story, the long version.

Granader Family Prize for Outstanding Writing Portfolio

The Spectrum Center: Enriching the Campus Experience

https://ritameih.wixsite.com/ritahathwriting100

by Rita Hathaway

From Writing 100

Nominated by Simone Sessolo

Rita's website on the Spectrum Center shows her excellent development in rhetorical strategies and multimodal composition. The website houses texts covering several writing genres: the personal essay, the interview, the annotated bibliography, and the argumentative essay. Plus, it compliments these texts with relevant information about an important campus service. The website is so excellently designed that the Spectrum Center itself should consider using it as a form of outreach. Rita shows that she has progressed to a level that allows her to excel in future writing classes at the University of Michigan.

Simone Sessolo

Uncovering Myself

According to the movie Pitch Perfect, one in ten women are lesbians (Pitch Perfect, 2012). Now, my high school's graduating class had about three-hundred fifty students. Let's say half of them identify as female. That would mean that there would be, at most, seventeen girls who also like girls. Subtract myself from that and you'd end up with sixteen lesbians in my grade. Now you might think, "oh, sixteen is a decent amount of lesbians, especially if there are sixteen per grade. You should eventually be able to find someone you feel compatible with." Well, let me also explain that in high school I did not socialize with that many people in my class, much less those in other grades. Also, a handful of these lesbians were not out publicly so unless you have an amazing gay-dar (which I sadly do not obtain), it was extremely hard to know who else was gay.

I am sad to say that throughout my four years of high school I fell for many straight girls. There was no way to avoid it because, as you would assume from my previous math, the straight girls outnumbered the gay ones by a substantial amount. And while this was often discouraging, it only confirmed my belief that I was into girls.

Let me backtrack a little bit and go through the quick summary of my young high school self just to give you a better sense of where I was at four short years ago. Freshmen year I was the typical annoying freshmen and I still cringe a lot just thinking back on that year. I tried too hard to fit in and be "popular" without having a good grasp on who I was and who I truly wanted to be. Sophomore year my personality practically did a 180 and I became quiet and timid. It wasn't until junior that I started to feel comfortable in my skin. By the beginning of the school year I had come out to my close friends and family and I was finally starting to accept who I was. Senior year I felt the most confident I had ever felt. People knew I was gay, even those who I hadn't told, but I didn't mind.

I was proud of who I was and people around me accepted me much quicker than I was able to accept myself.

But for a long time I felt lost. Confused. Worried that I would never feel comfortable in my own skin and envying people that were. You might be feeling this same way. But please, believe me when I say it will get better. It takes time to realize who you are and what you like. There's going to be some pitfalls along the way but just know, you won't feel so lonely and confused forever. At some point it will all start to make sense. And I'm not saying I have all my life together but I can tell you that that feeling of belonging I so yearned for four years ago has started to become reality.

Now with this is mind it wasn't until junior year that I found a solid group of friends that I could relate with when it came to sexuality. Maybe there is some underlying force that makes bi/lesbian girls gravitate towards one another because I found that three of these sixteen girls were some of my best friends. That was great. We talked about Emma Watson (I LOVE Emma Watson, in the gay way), and television shows with lesbian characters. We were all able to connect (on both a personal and a gay level) and I was finally able to express a part of myself that I had kept hidden for the majority of my life.

Even though there were only four of us and we didn't always see each other due to our busy schedules I liked that sense of belonging. I liked being able to be completely myself. That is the type of community I am looking for now.

The Spectrum Center offers a safe place for any student who faces the ultimate question of "who am I." Whether that is dealing with sexual orientation or gender, the Spectrum Center helps to give LGBTQ+ students a place where we can be unapologetically ourselves.

I recently visited the Spectrum Center, unsure of what to expect. My school had a similar group called the GSA (Gay Straight Alliance) which

I tried but never officially joined because even though it was a group of queer students I did not feel like I belonged. But to my surprise, I felt very comfortable in the Spectrum Center. I was able to meet a bunch of new people and connect with them, not only through the fact that we were all not straight, but also just as people. I really enjoyed the community and I felt that sense of belonging that I had found with my solid group junior year and lacked when trying to join the GSA.

The group reminded me that there were others like me and that I wasn't alone. I think that it's important, especially at big universities like U of M, to be reminded of the comradery between people and to find the place where there are others that share your interests. I think that the Spectrum Center would help continue to build my confidence in myself and also be a good way to meet people who are similar to me. I enjoy being in a place where the ratio of queer girls is greater than one to ten. Really, at the Spectrum Center the ratio is most likely ten to ten.

I encourage you, if you're feeling alone and confused about your sexuality, gender, or any aspect of the LGBTQ+ community, to come and join the Spectrum Center with me. Let's get rid of the math and the numbers and the ratios. Let's find a place where we make the majority. Where we feel comfortable being ourselves.

Spectrum Center: A Home Within a Home
Finding a place to fit in as students identifying as LGBTQ+

Michigan Union: Spectrum Center is on the Third Floor

When you first get to Michigan and walk the city streets of Ann Arbor it might feel overwhelming. The University of Michigan is a large campus with thousands of students walking through the diag each day. There are so many new people to meet and it's hard to know where exactly you'll fit in, especially as a student who identifies as LGBTQ+. But if you find yourself at the Union, head up to the third floor and you'll find a place called the Spectrum Center, a place specifically designated for students who identify as LGBTQ+.

The Spectrum Center is made to be "a welcoming and cozy environment for all the LGBTQ+ students and staff" says Mark Chung Kwan Fan, the Assistant Director for Engagement at the Center. "There is a lounge where people can just chill out and have conversations" and "students come back there to do homework and have lunch during lunchtime hours." Around 2,700 students visited the

Mark Chung Kwan Fan

Spectrum Center in 2016 and this year they are hoping the numbers will increase.

Mark Chung Kwan Fan also mentions that the Spectrum Center offers weekly activities, including free HIV rapid testing and centers spaces. He says that center spaces are "support groups that are non therapeutical with folks who have different identities." There is a queer and trans people of color space, as well as trans non binary space, bi/pansexual/fluid space, and a general LGBTQ+ space. These center spaces allow students to come together and share experiences, daily challenges, and an overall sense of community.

"We strive to create as an inclusive community for the LGBTQ+ students as we can"

Everyone is welcome at the Spectrum Center regardless of gender identity or sexuality. The staff is very diverse, coming from many different backgrounds and identifying in different ways. This is extremely helpful for students who want to be able to connect with someone who they can relate to. There is also a mentorship program between staff and students that is a private, flexible process

Entrance of Spectrum Center

and allows students, whether they are out or not, to connect with someone who has been in their shoes and can understand where they're coming from.

"The Spectrum Center welcomes anybody regardless of gender identity or sexuality"

The assistant director also informed me that "All of the staff are trained in bystander intervention so should problematic challenges arise we [the staff] will know how to address that." He says that especially right now he knows "it's hard to promise a safe and inclusive space, but that the Spectrum Center strives towards being able to provide that" for all students and staff. There are gender neutral bathrooms on the third floor of the union as well as in some dorms, which is just a small part of how the Spectrum Center and U of M are trying to make campus more inclusive and safe.

Mark Chung Kwan Fan says that the staff and the center also really "value peer-to-peer relationships, that is the student-to-student relationships." The Spectrum Center often hosts events during times that are celebrated throughout the nation such as during national coming out week and trans awareness week. These activities allow LGBTQ+ students to meet one another and bond over the same shared pride for the community. This helps make the campus a little bit smaller and allows students with different sexual orientations and gender identities to come together and find a loving community.

"There is a lounge where people can just chill out and have conversations"

At the Spectrum Center there is "a mantra of empathy." The staff aim to relate with the students and one of the great aspects about the Spectrum Center is the staff try and learn about the person as a whole, past just their sexuality and/or gender identity. The people in the Spectrum Center know that every student has a story and that each story is unique, they then use this knowledge and try to "address all of the students' social identities." This really allows for the student to find people who are similar to them in more ways than one and allows the staff members to gain a better understanding of the student, creating a better relationship between everyone.

Staff and Students Coming Together as a Community

To Mark Chung Kwan Fan there are so many great parts about the Spectrum Center and he values them all. If he had to choose he would say that his favorite part is the people because "people bring such authenticity to the center, whether they are staff or students. Being able to interact with students and really understand the different stories and backgrounds they're coming from is my [Mark Chung Kwan Fan] favorite part." He says that "It's not all about helping, but more about connecting with them [the students]." Overall it is very evident that the Spectrum Center is more than just a name: it is a loving, caring community that, if you want it to be, can definitely become your home within the home at the University of Michigan.

The Spectrum Center: A Place for Vigorous Debate

The University of Michigan is known for its well-rounded programs and strong academic reputation. Thousands of students are admitted each year from many different walks of life, which is what brings such diversity to the campus. Yet, with thousands of students in each graduating class and even more on the entire campus it can be hard to find a place to fit in, especially as a student identifying as LGBTQ+. Overall U of M is an inclusive community, but it can be hard to find people who share similar backgrounds and experiences. A community within Michigan that can help to bring together students identifying as LGBTQ+ is the Spectrum Center. The Spectrum Center was created in March of 1970 right after the Detroit Gay Liberation Movement, and at that time it was a very small organization on campus. Since then the Spectrum Center has grown into a well known and large community that helps students of all gender identities and sexualities find a safe space on campus. As a student identifying as Lesbian, I believe that the Spectrum Center is a great place for LGBTQ+ students to connect and bond with others who share similar experiences, it also is a great place to grow in character and confidence as not only a student but also as an overall person.

Official Spectrum Center Website

There are multiple aspects to why it's important to have a space on campus where LGBTQ+ students can feel safe to be themselves. One reason is that it is an inclusive community that supports and includes all students, no matter their sexual orientation or gender identity. Mark Chung Kwan Fan, the assistant director at the Spectrum Center, explains how the staff within the center really "value peer-to-peer relationships, that is the student-to-student relationships." This aspect of the center really emphasizes how close the community is and how important creating connections and relationships with other students is. This feeling of community and friendship is a large aspect of what makes the Spectrum Center so important for students identifying as LGBTQ+. It can be difficult to find other students to relate to on the subject of sexuality and identity, but the Spectrum Center makes it easy for students to connect with peers that can empathize and understand.

Another reason that is important to have a Spectrum Center on campus is that the support can help to improve mental and emotional health when people decide to disclose their sexual orientation. According to Rebecca Lester, in her article Coming Out is a Healthy Decision, coming out helps to improve the overall health of a person identifying as LGBTQ+. She explains how not only does "emotional and mental health improve" after someone is able to come out, but also "the level of stress that is associated with hiding [sexual orientation] is reduced." This helps to convey the importance of having a space where people are comfortable being themselves and embracing their sexuality and/or gender identity. Not only does a safe space improve health, but it also allows student to reduce their stress levels. This is very important because college students already have a large amount of stress due to classwork, time management, and the basic responsibilities of living alone. Add on the stress of feeling the need to hide sexuality/gender identity and that creates an unhealthy and ineffective work environment. These reasons emphasize the importance of having the Spectrum Center on campus and available for students identifying as LGBTQ+. The community allows for students to embrace who they are and therefore grow as a student and a person.

The Spectrum Center doesn't only help to improve physical and emotional wellbeing but it also helps to educate the larger community and create more understanding and empathy from students who aren't queer. According to Juliet

Guichon, in the article Alliances Make School Life Safer; Benefits of Gay-straight Clubs Proven, creating spaces for LGBTQ+ students also decreases the amount of harassment that comes from their straight peers. After the addition of a Gay Straight Alliance (GSA) in one school, students found "that homophobic slurs ha[d] 'dramatically' decreased [...] 'nobody comes by and yells 'fag' or anything.'" This helps to illustrate how clubs such as GSA and the Spectrum Center help to educate the broader public and decrease homophobia. This is a benefit to not only LGBTQ+ students but also the community in general.

Michigan Spectrum Center Logo

Erin Petrow, in the article Gay Straight Alliance Helps Create Safe Spaces; Students from Across Province to Attend Summit, reiterates the importance of having GSA's within schools due to both the benefits for LGBTQ+ students and the overall community. There is an emphasis on the importance of schools as not only a place "where we receive an education, [but also a place] where we find community and gay straight alliances are an easy and obvious way to do that." This helps to convey how GSAs are great spaces for students to make friends and bond with one another. The Spectrum Center, which is similar to a Gay Straight Alliance, has the same intent: to make a safe and inclusive environment for students to meet people they can relate to and be unapologetically themselves. The article also mentions that safe spaces, such as a Gay Straight Alliance or the Spectrum Center, help to enlighten the general public and can lead to a safer school overall. It was found that "schools with a GSA in place for three years or longer actually saw a reduction in bullying rates - for all students, not only those who identify on the LGBTQ spectrum" (Petrow). This emphasizes the importance of the Spectrum Center and portrays how the services from the organization positively affect the entire community.

While safe spaces are beneficial to students, some people question whether safe spaces actually improve the overall education of the nation as a whole. According to the Celine Cooper's article Squaring 'Safe Space' and Free Speech; Universities Must Foster Respectful Dialogue, Make Students Think, safe spaces can prevent important dialogue on topics that need to be discussed more often. Cooper believes that an important aspect of a university education is to "connect with the real world and with the material realities of people's lives," but that universities are also "the last places [to] look for vigorous debate, least of all sensitive topic[s]" because there is a layer of sensitivity when it comes to certain topics, such as LGBTQ+ rights in an LGBTQ+ safe space (Cooper). While this is an understandable concern and a very important issue, the Spectrum Center is not a place where the thoughts and opinions of varying views are not allowed to be spoken, people are not meant to be silenced within the doors of the community. However, because the center is meant to be an inclusive space for students identifying as LGBTQ+ there will be a strong reaction to anything negative about the center or the people within it. The Spectrum Center is not meant to be a place that forbids discussion on difficult topics, but they do want to create a space where students feel that they can express themselves without fear of being ridiculed or dehumanized.

While I believe that discussions on sensitive topics are very important and lead to future changes and societal improvements, I also think that it is important for students who feel marginalized and different to have a place to go to feel safe and confident with who they are. This is what allows students to feel comfortable to discuss these difficult topics. What Cooper did not understand is that vigorous debate can thrive in environments such as the Spectrum Center. These safe spaces, allow different views to be expressed in a respectful and comfortable environment. The comradery within the community makes it easier to speak and listen to other opinions as well as gain a better understanding for an opposing belief. It does not have to include bigoted and hateful views in order to be valid. The Spectrum Center is a place that supports the LGBTQ+ community as well as allies. This community is a good learning environment because of the diversity. It is a space in which allies and other students can become more educated on topics and issues that the LGBTQ+ community faces.

It took me a long time to come to terms with my sexuality. I was lucky to not have anyone close to me in my life talk poorly about the LGBTQ+ community, but I still had many of my own insecurities to overcome. I felt like even though no one was against me liking the same gender there was still no one I could talk to about it who would understand what I was feeling and going through. I think that is what is so great about the Spectrum Center, it gives me a place to not only feel comfortable being myself but to meet many more students who are also queer. It is a great feeling knowing that I have that community behind me and that there are others on campus who I can relate to about my sexuality. For students who feel that they are struggling to find others who can relate on topics of sexual orientation and gender identity I would highly recommend checking out the Spectrum Center. It is an easy and helpful way to meet other students who are going through or have been through similar experiences and can relate to the struggle of needing to deal with sexuality and gender identity as well as any other aspects of your identity such as race, religion, ethnicity, etc. It can be difficult to balance all of your identities, especially if they send conflicting messages, but the Spectrum Center is a great place to go and find support.

The Spectrum Center at the University of Michigan is an inclusive space for students identifying as LGBTQ+ to come together and meet others with similar backgrounds. It is an important community on campus and can help students who are struggling with understanding and accepting their sexuality and/ or gender identity. It is also a place where students can express and be themselves without worrying about being judged. The Spectrum Center is a great place for students who want to further their own self-confidence as well as meet other students who share similar experiences.

Works Cited

Cooper, Celine. "Squaring 'Safe Spaces' and Free Speech; Universities Must Foster Respectful Dialogue Make Students Think." The Gazette, 18 Apr. 2014, p. A6.

Guichon, Juliet. "Alliances Make School Life Safer; Benefits of Gay-Straight Clubs Proven." The Calgary Herald, 16 Dec. 2014, p. B7.

Lester, Rebecca. "Coming Out' is a Healthy Decision." Toronto Star Newspaper, 06 Oct. 2010, p. WR5.

Petrow, Erin. "Gay Straight Alliance Helps Create Safe Spaces; Students from Across Province to Attend Summit." The Leader-Post, 17 Nov. 2017, p. A9.

Past/Future of My Home

https://yinghwu.wordpress.com/
by Ying-Hsuan Wu
From Writing 100
Nominated by Jimmy Brancho

I challenged my students to take a stand on a controversial topic this term in Writing 100, and Ying-Hsuan took up the complex issue of Taiwan's independence. She wrote well-informed, balanced pieces throughout the term and made excellent progress in examining the situation separately from her personal bias. However, where this portfolio truly shines, I feel, is in a beautiful personal essay that begins with a personal account of a summer family trip and ends with a call to action. Ying-Hsuan blends these two goals seamlessly. My goal for my students was to create personal essays that led the reader into their issue of choice, and Ying-Hsuan's heartfelt "Summer in Tainan" is exemplary.

Jimmy Brancho

Independence or Unification?

Preface:

In the op-ed, the authors are more free, and unlike the academic papers, they are allowed to voice their own thoughts in the paper and be opinionated. However, in order to not let the readers think I am biased regarding this topic, I accompanied some of the evidences from my researched argument paper and the story from my personal essay into this op-ed. Although this is the one genre without many guidelines and the requirement of a thesis statement, I think it is the hardest one among all the writings we did in this term. At first, I did not know where to start writing because of op-ed's comparative lack of structure. Even though it is a good news that I did not have find all the sources all over again, the organization of the paper tends to be a bit hard since it is a combination of both personal stories and evidences from my previous two papers. Moreover, I did struggle in following the style of the op-eds I read in class since I was not sure when is the most appropriate time to start a new paragraph to emphasize the most important ideas but at the same time not disturbing the flow and connection of the paragraphs. However, I do think that compare to the researched argument paper, the readers might be able to find this piece much more stronger and interesting to read since there is a clear stand on an issue and instead of dull statistics and research, it incorporates personal opinions and stories. I did enjoy writing this essay since this is the kind of genre that I did not get a chance to try before.

Born and raised in Taiwan, I consider it as my home.

This identity of mine reminds me of my first day on campus for the international orientation. The one thing that I remembered the most from the event is not the impressment of the size of the campus, not the diversity of the student body, not the excitement of meeting new friends, and definitely not the dull presentations we had all day long. But rather a single small event that happened in the beginning of the welcoming speech: country roll call. I was not surprised when over half of the people in the auditorium stood up when the speaker announced China, but as the "t" slowly approached, my heart started to pound hardly.

The conflict between China and Taiwan is never a new one and can be traced back to 1949. Originally the ruling government of China, Nationalist Party (KMT) lost the civil War against the Communist Party led by Mao and was forced to retreat to the island, hoping one day that they would be able to fight back. Unfortunately, KMT never succeeded and though two sides have been governed separately ever since, the intense relationship between the two sides remained with China claiming Taiwan as part of its territory and Taiwan asserting itself as a sovereign state.

By: Rodrigo[https://www.toonpool.com/cartoons/Year%20of%20the%20Monkey%20in%20 Taiwan_264275]

Even though cultural, historical, and linguistic heritages mostly endure, there exists a good reason why unification remains unpopular among the Taiwanese people. Externally, people pay close attention to Beijing's claim to almost entire

South China Sea and Hong Kong's struggle in choosing its own representative candidates. Internally, people felt the threat posed by approximately 700 missiles currently pointed toward the small island, even after years of increasing concord under President Ma and Nationalist Party's rule.

It seems like the road toward independence is inevitable as many citizens in Taiwan share this same feeling and self-identity. By 2014, only 3 percent of the population still regard themselves exclusively as Chinese. Nearly 90% of the students, ranging from middle to high school, see themselves as Taiwanese. If this trend continues, a sole Taiwanese identity will prevail in the society.

Moreover, Taiwan's well functioned democracy contrasts sharply with China's communism. Last year, Tsai Ing-Wen, a candidate from the pro-independence Democratic Progressive Party (DPP) was elected as the first female president with historic landslide victory, marking an important turning point in Taiwan's history. In her inaugural speech, she contributed her victory to people's [commitment] to the defense of our freedom and democratic way of life".

It is really hard to imagine what life would be like if our rights of speech, universal suffrage, and freedom are taken away. We Taiwanese people grew up viewing these as our inalienable rights. This democratic government of ours has always been something that we are proud of. It may not be the most effective system, but it is a symbol of freedom, in which all men's voices are valued and heard. As the only democratic government in Chinese speaking country, this institution of ours is the backbone of the nation and represents what we are made of. If "returning" means giving up all these rights and identities, then for sure unification is not the most suitable option for the people in Taiwan.

I cannot stop imagining what it would be like if China does take over Taiwan just like what they did decades ago to Hong Kong. Will Taiwan be the same? Will this beloved island of mine still be my home? I guess not. In every aspect, we are just too different to be the same. Even with an island as small as Taiwan can contain cities with various characteristics, how many differences can we possibly have as we compare Taiwan to China?

Though China's "One country, Two Systems" plan tries to combat this particular difference, Hong King's internal struggles under the hypothetical framework diminishes Taiwan's confidence and hope in remaining the status quo under the Communist party. 50 years of autonomy had been promised before the return. However, in less than 25 years, the promises had been broken. Elections are manipulated in favor of pro-Beijing candidates with zero democratic substance. People helplessly see freedom slowly slips through their hands as they expressed their resentment and disappointment through a mass protest famously known as the Umbrella Movement in 2014. Unfortunately, under the cover of a prosperous financial center in Asia, this is the cruel reality of Hong Kong's current state.

By: Kei Sze, [http://www.projects.socialsciences.manchester.ac.uk/global-social-challenges/2017/06/01/radicalisation-among-young-people-in-hong-kong/]15465630910_f2c5927c65_b

Flickr, by: Studio Incendo [https://www.flickr.com/photos/studiokanu/15465630910]

Moreover, unlike what most people expected, evidences show that remaining strong economic ties with China is no longer benefiting Taiwan, but rather hurting it since the mainland's economy is slowing down. In 2014, Taiwan's government promised that its economy would grow and expand at least 3%, however, the goal was never achieved due to the mainland's decreasing demand on numerous products, specifically high-tech goods. This causes a lot of concerns regarding the future economy of the island.

The trade agreement Economic Cooperation Framework Agreement (ECFA) established with China that aims to stimulate economy under the previous president also turned out to be a failure as it "undermines the autonomy of Taiwan, threatens the employment of Taiwanese laborers and farmers, and cause over-dependence on the Chinese market". This plan, though at first seemed promising, turned out to be an economic failure, stirring much political and social unrest in Taiwan. The disappointment toward the government and resentment for the failure of ECFA soon led to the famous Sunflower Movement as the protesters occupied the parliament for 24 days, denouncing the government's overly China-friendly stand.

Wikipedia: [https://en.wikipedia.org/wiki/Sunflower_Student_Movement]

Flickr, By: Artemas Liu [https://www.flickr.com/photos/north_blue/13798324494]

The independence of Taiwan is a very sensitive issue. And the fate of the island is not definite yet as Taiwanese people's reaction and preferences depends largely on how the Chinese government act and treat with problem of growing disparities between the two regions. However, after all those protests I saw on the news, all the unfairness we experienced, and the precious memories I created with my friends and families in Taiwan, they culminated in an epiphany.

I am proud of being a Taiwanese.

Even when it means that we will not be able to sing our national anthem in any international event. Even when it means that we will always be known as Chinese Taipei or Republic of China but never as Taiwan. Even when it means that we cannot take seats in UN. Even when it means that we will not be able to proudly wave our flags. Even when it means that we will continue to face the constant military and diplomatic pressure from our neighbor. Still, I am proud of being a Taiwanese, and always will be. It is my root and where I belong.

No matter how long the fight of gaining recognition will take, Taiwanese people will always stand up for it, just like how the citizens respond to China's increasing ambition and pressure with their commitment to democracy through last year's presidential election and just like how I stood up that day in the auditorium when the word "Taiwan" was finally announced. I, alongside with other Taiwanese students, stood up without hesitation and accept the applause with pride. This is the most silent, but bravest rebellion I have ever done in my life.

Fate of the Island

Preface:

In academic writings, the author's personal voice and opinions tend not to be the focus. Basically, this genre let the evidences do the main talking. This not only can make the writing more credible, but can also prevent the readers from feeling that the author is biased in the firsthand. At first, I find this particularly hard since I am obviously biased in this matter. As a person living in Taiwan for 18 years, this intense political atmosphere and conflict was nothing special and was present in my everyday life. Even so, I tried to avoid bias by including some quotations from credible sources and data from numerous surveys in the paper to better back up the points I made. I paid attention on using words and phrases that are less strong and let the evidences lead the readers to the conclusion that Taiwan should not continue to keep close relationship with China. Another challenge I faced is to organize a 10-page writing, allowing it to run and transition smoothly from one point to the other. This is a place where I spend a lot of time on, revising many times to try to find a best way to present my points in a clear and logical way. Constructing a thesis statement for such a long paper is also quite difficult. At first I buried it pretty far down, but readers might not be able to get my main message immediately; therefore, I later made some revisions of it as well by moving to the last sentence of the first paragraph, grabbing readers' attention and interest in the beginning of the writing.

Taiwan has become increasingly close with China economically for the past few years as over half of the foreign investments and goods end up in China, greatly contributing to the growth of Taiwan's economy. However, some actions taken by the Chinese government still prevent it from winning the hearts of people in Taiwan. Externally, people saw the struggles of Hong Kong to fight the right to choose their own representative candidates from Beijing. Internally, people pay close attention to Beijing's claim to almost entire South China Sea. They also felt the threat posed by approximately 700 missiles currently pointed toward the small island, even after years of increasing concord under President Ma and Nationalist Party's rule. With this mixed feeling toward China, which side will the Taiwanese people choose ultimately, unification or independence? With Taiwanese people's self-identity and Hong Kong's current political and social unrest under China's "One Country, Two Systems" framework, Taiwanese people may not find keeping close relationship with China that beneficial, especially without good economic incentives.

It seems that people are currently leaning toward the side of independence as the citizens expressed their thoughts through the presidential election last year. With historic landslide victory, Tsai Ing-Wen, a candidate from the pro-independence Democratic Progressive Party (DPP) was elected as the first female president, marking an important turning point in Taiwan's history. The party also for the first time controlled the majority of the legislature. In her inaugural speech, she contributed her victory to people's "[commitment] to the defense of our freedom and democratic way of life" (Chen).

*Wikimedia Commons: [https://commons.wikimedia.org/wiki/File:2008TaiwanPresidentialElection_*
Celebrations_from_Ma%27s_Supporters.jpg]
Wikimedia Commons: [https://commons.wikimedia.org/wiki/File:Tsai_Ing-wen_20170613.jpg]

The conflict and intense relationship between China and Taiwan is never a new one and can be traced back to 1949. Originally the ruling government of China, Nationalist Party (KMT) lost the civil War against the Communist Party led by Mao and was forced to retreat to the island, hoping one day they would be able to fight back. However, KMT never succeeded and the two sides have been governed separately ever since. Based on the historical standpoint, one can understand why the Beijing government views Taiwan as part of its territory, but the main reason behind China's strong assertion is, in fact, due to geographical and political concerns. To prevent America's further influence in Asia and Pacific regions, it is very unlikely that the Chinese government will give up Taiwan and recognize its independence.

Even though a common cultural, historical, and linguistic heritages mostly endure, Taiwan's well-functioned democracy contrasts sharply with China's communism. With the history of three democratic turnover of power, Taiwan holds the only democratic government in the Chinese speaking world and is one of the most progressive country in Asia, with access to universal suffrage, and freedom of speech and publication. How is it possible that the people in Taiwan are willing to sacrifice all these rights and rejoin the mainland? Seeing and recognizing this as one of the main obstacle toward achieving unification, China, therefore, proposed the "One Country, Two Systems" framework. This plan basically tried to win Taiwanese people's trust and confidence by guaranteeing that the island would be able to preserve its political system and remain the status quo as long as it does not challenge the authority of the Chinese government (King). However, before Taiwanese people agreed with the plan, Hong Kong turned out to be the little mouse in this great experiment first when it was returned by Britain to China in 1991, testing the reliability of the promises granted by the Chinese government. Since then, Taiwan paid keen attention to the events that happened in Hong Kong as it might be the future of the island if it does rejoin the mainland.

By: MISTER BIJOU [http://misterbijou.blogspot.com/2006/07/]

Sadly, this proposed system after 20 years of testing seemed to disappoint not only Hong Kong but also diminishes Taiwan's confidence in keeping the status quo and autonomy under this hypothetical framework. In an interview with Matthew, an assistant professor at the University of Hong Kong, people can get a brief understanding of some internal struggles Hong Kong is facing under the "One Country, Two Systems" plan. It turns out that the things people in Hong Kong long valued, such as "freedom, rule of law, and the lack of corruption, seem to be slowly eroding" (Wong). Though he recognizes that China did a good job in ensuring Hong Kong's economic freedom and competitiveness in Asia, he also mentions the fact that Beijing now mainly controls Hong Kong's capital, properties, and economy. The most urging concern, however, is China's increasing control over Hong Kong politically, breaking its original promise of granting Hong Kong 50 years of autonomy. Hong Kong people widely expect full democracy, but the suffrage proposal China offered is anything but democratic (King). Though the plan includes popular vote, the nomination of candidates is carefully monitored and selected so that the ballot would be limited to solely pro-Beijing candidates, with zero democratic substance. This constant oppression soon led to strong opposition and the famous Umbrella Movement in 2014. Though the proposal was quickly voted down, this does not change the fact that China had failed to keep its promise, causing political and social unrest in Hong Kong under the "One Country, Two Systems" framework. After all these incidences and struggles Hong Kong experienced, the survey conducted in 2002 suggested the fact that only approximately 10 percent of Taiwanese saw the proposed system as a workable plan for Taiwan (Popham). If Hong Kong turns out to be a failed example of the plan, it is very unlikely that Taiwanese people will be convinced that their way of life would not be disturbed under the rule of the Chinese government, even with generous deals and promises.

In addition, as the two regions develop further and further away from each other, more people begin to identify themselves as Taiwanese rather than Chinese. In the 1990s, when the island became a democracy, about 25 percent of the people recognize themselves as exclusively Chinese and those who identified themselves as exclusively Taiwanese barely reached one fourth of the population (Chen). However, by 2014, only 3 percent still regard themselves exclusively as Chinese. This is a drastic change in how residents in Taiwan identify themselves in less than 25 years. Moreover, a survey conducted last year by China Youth Corps discovered that nearly 90% of the students, ranging from middle to high school, see themselves as Taiwanese. If this trend continues, a sole Taiwanese identity will prevail in the society as "people grow even more adamant about the island's separate entity" (Sui). All these numbers and statistics suggest that even if China one day does decide to gain Taiwan by force, the country will never be truly unified since Taiwanese people's hearts do not reside with the Chinese government and hold different opinions regarding their self-identity.

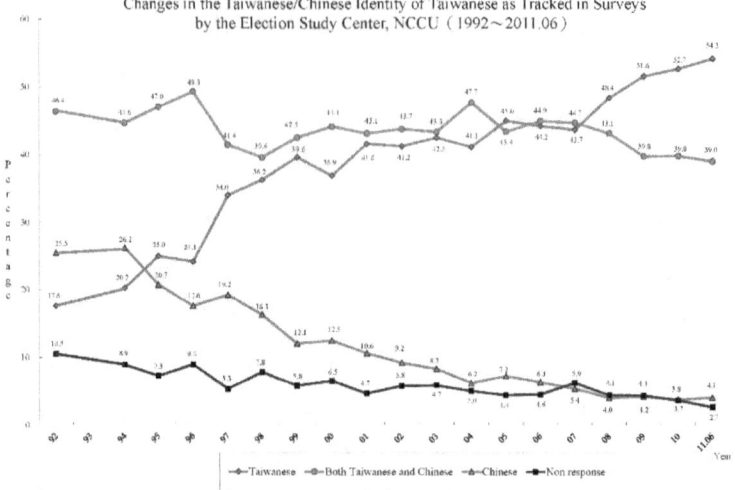

By: Woodrow W. Clark [http://taiwancorner.org/?p=1167]

However, when it comes to the problem of gaining independence and recognizing Taiwan as a country, the nearly unanimous opinion no longer exists. With this question, one must weigh more than just their self-identity, but the future of the island socially, economically, and politically. It is about the safety of the people when taking the missiles currently pointing at the island into consideration. It is about all the small companies in Taiwan that rely heavily on their trades with China. It is always good to have a sense of patriotism, but it is also equally important to think of the consequences before taking actions. And this is the reason why most people in Taiwan are divided in this matter.

For the past decades, Emerson Niou, a political scientist at Duke University, has interviewed with numerous citizens in Taiwan with randomized phone calls (Popham). These surveys depicted that about 75 percent of the people who participated in interviews would support Taiwanese independence if China will not respond by attacking Taiwan. For Taiwanese younger than 40, pro-independence support reaches 84 percent. However, when considering all the possible costs of reaching independence, around "80 percent of the people chose bread over romance and supports remaining economic ties with China" (Chen).

Therefore, under President Ma's administration from 2008, Taiwan became actively establishing economic ties with China, hoping cooperation could improve Taiwan's economy and create a less intense and more friendly and stable relationship with its neighbor. A landmark trade agreement, Economic Cooperation Framework Agreement (ECFA), was created with a good intention. The Nationalist Party expected it would "promote domestic growth, prevent marginalization, and encourage trade agreements with other countries" (Chou), opening Taiwan to the global market. This plan, though at first seemed promising and would stimulate Taiwan's economy greatly, later turned out to be an economic failure, stirring much political and social unrest in Taiwan. In fact, it "undermines the autonomy of Taiwan, threatens the employment of Taiwanese laborers and farmers, and cause overdependence on the Chinese market" (Chou). Though President Ma asserted that this was a mere economic cooperation, there is no guarantee that this seemingly pure economic cooperation will result in zero political implications. With economic relation so close with China, about 65 percent of people in Taiwan fear that they are handing over too much of the island's control to China (Makinen). And this influence China gained through economic activities will one day be used as a weapon against Taiwan itself.

Letters from Taiwan: [http://lettersfromtaiwan.tw/post/41886535288/
taipei-times-cartoon-depicting-one-view-of-the-ma]

Because of China's big market and low cost in its workers and laborers, more and more Taiwanese businesses transitioned parts of their operating stations to China for these past few years (Chou). As a result, more than two million Taiwanese businessmen live in China due to this reason. This not only means that Taiwan is losing valuable human resources, but also means that the employers in Taiwan was largely affected as many businesses move oversea to seek cheaper laborers. More importantly, Taiwan enjoys advantage over China because of its advanced technologies and expertise, but because ECFA opened the market between two sides, technologies can be learned by the Chinese. Taiwan in return will lose its advantage and competitiveness in the global market. Thus, limit Taiwan's development and economy.

These facts all depict that ECFA is more of a failure rather than a success. However, still many people hold faith within the potential of the Chinese market. They see remaining strong economic ties with China, where higher wages and more opportunities are provided, as crucial to the development of the small island. However, sadly, this belief is no longer true as the research and reports suggest that China's economy is, in fact, slowing down. On one side, this might seem to be a devastating news since Taiwan has been seriously affected, but on the other side this can also be considered as a great opportunity to seek for new trading partners and stop Taiwan's reliance on the Chinese market. Research found that though China's economy had been growing rapidly for the past few decades, it has relied on what the International Monetary Fund calls an "unsustainable growth model, based on excessive loans and investments, that has created big risks in the banking, real estate and corporate sectors" since the 2008 global financial crisis (Makinene).

In 2014, Taiwan's government promised that its economy will grow and expand at least 3%, however, the goal was never achieved due to the mainland's decreasing demand on numerous products, specifically high-tech goods (Makinen). When it became clear that the economy, even after sacrificing some degree of autonomy and the welfare of Taiwanese employers, had still not improved much, anti-Chinese government sentiment and pro-independence sound grew louder and louder. This soon led to the famous Sunflower Movement, which is the largest anti-China demonstration in years. The protesters occupied the parliament for 24 days, denouncing Ma's China-friendly stand (Sui). As a result, the government was forced to pass and agree on a new law in allowing more public oversight of negotiations with Beijing. Though the majority of the people resented government's failed promise of recovering economy, the protest itself, however, was very controversial as some people view it as too violent and disrespectful. Nonetheless, it still shows people's concern in keeping close economic ties with China.

The independence of Taiwan is a very sensitive issue and every step should be taken after careful considerations. It seems like people are now leaning toward independence even under China's increasing ambition. This can be seen through people's self-identification and their growing resentment in the continued economic recession even after their dependence on the Chinese market. Furthermore, Hong Kong's internal struggles also decreases people's willingness to rejoin the mainland since the proposed system does not seem to work on Taiwan. The fate of the island is not definite yet as Taiwanese people's reaction and preferences depends largely on how China treats the problem of growing disparities between the two regions. However, with those reasons mentioned above, it currently seems unlikely that the unification can be achieved in the near future.

Work Cited:

Chen, Fang-Yu. "The Taiwanese see themselves as Taiwanese, not as Chinese."
The *Washington Post*, 2 Jan. Web. 12 Oct. 2017.

Chou, Chi-An. "A Two-Edged Sword: The Economy Cooperation Framework
Agreement Between the Republic of China and the People's Republic of
China" *BYU Law Library*, n.d. Web. 12 Oct. 2017.

King, Sean. "China's 'One Country, Two Systems' Principle Won't Ever Work In
Taiwan." *Forbes*, 25 Jun. 2017. Web. 11 Oct. 2017.

Makinen, Julie. "China has been showing signs of economic slowdown, trade
partners say." *Los Angeles Times*, 26 Aug. 2015. Web. 13 Oct. 2017.

Popham, Peter. "Twenty years on, Taiwan is still struggling to shake off China's
embrace." *Independent.co.uk*, 15 Jan. 2016. Web. 12 Oct. 2017/

Sui, Cindy. "Will the Sunflower Movement change Taiwan?" *BBC*, 9 Apr. 2015.
Web. 11 Oct. 2017.

Wong, Mathew. "Is Hong Kong Losing its Identity?" *THE CIPHER BRIEF*, 30
Jun. 2017. Web. 12 Oct. 2017.

Summer in Tainan

Preface:

I wrote this personal essay in a storytelling way, recalling one of the most memorable family trip to visit my grandparents. There is no conversation throughout the entire piece and the essay mainly focuses on what I personally see and feel, but I did include many descriptive languages to allow the readers to create vivid images in their minds as they read the paper. The parallelisms I incorporated function the same way since they are helpful in emphasizing the main ideas. In the opening of the paper, I mentioned a short event that happened recently to attract readers' attention and lead them to my main topic. For the majority of the paper, then , I discussed my family trip to Tainan, which is a city in southern Taiwan. Through this personal experience of this particularly memorable family trip, I hope readers will be able to understand how I am emotionally attached to this island that I am lucky enough to call home. The concluding sentence of the piece also links back to the story I told in the very beginning of the paper about the event, allowing the readers to know that I will always take actions when it comes to this issue. Near the end of the writing, I also addressed and expressed my personal opinions toward the issue of political conflict between Taiwan and China, making a better transition to my next paper, which is the researched essay about the relationship and conflict between Taiwan and China.

The one thing that sticks in my mind since the five-day international orientation might be very different from other people's answers. It is not the impressment of the size of the campus, not the diversity of the student body, not the excitement of meeting new friends, and definitely not the dull presentations we had all day long. But rather a single small event that happened in the beginning of the welcoming speech: country roll call. I was not surprised when over half of the people in the auditorium stood up when the speaker announced China, but as the "t" slowly approached, my heart started to pound hardly. "What if we are not being called?" "What if they don't consider us as a country?" The intense atmosphere surrounding my fellow Taiwanese friends and I finally disappeared after we heard the word "Taiwan". With no further hesitation, not even with the murmurs behind our backs, we stood up as Taiwanese and accept the applause with pride. This is the most silent, but bravest rebellion I have ever done in my life.

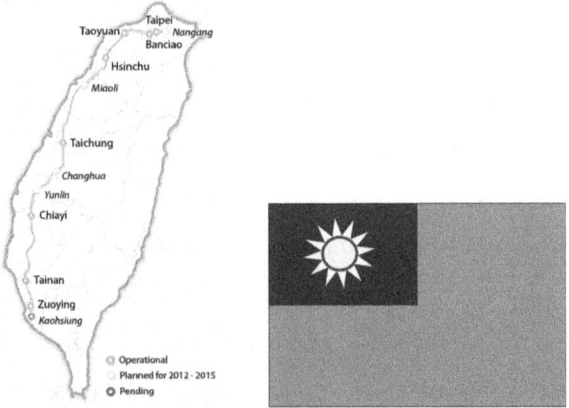

wikepedia: [https://zh.wikipedia.org/wiki/User:Infomark12/highway_en]
pixabay: [https://pixabay.com/zh/国旗-台湾-官方-中华民国-国家-亚洲-31015/]

Born and raised in Taipei, which is the capital of Taiwan, I consider it as my root and my home. Despite all the cultural and historical similarities and connections we share with China, I identify myself as a Taiwanese. As an international student, studying thousands of miles away from home is not an easy thing. The one time when homesickness hit me hard, I stared at the ceiling and wandered back to the good old days I spent with my dearest families on that beautiful island, hoping to seek some comfort to chase away loneliness and pressure.

The weather was beautiful that day I remember. Afternoon probably. My family and I headed south to visit Tainan, which is 4-hour ride away from Taipei and where my grandparents lived. Compare to my hometown, the view in Tainan was nothing alike. Fast moving cars, busy pedestrians, and the soaring skyscrapers were replaced by endless farmlands extended to the horizon. I was amazed. For the first time, I felt the sweetness of nature in the air. Closing my eyes, I can feel the swift breeze passing me by whispering with their own mysterious language. For the first time in my life, buildings did not block my view and a square chunk of sky was no longer the only scene I saw when I look up. For the first time, the nature was no longer irrelevant. It may sound ridiculous, but at that moment, I did feel as if I owned the sky and this whole world. Twenty minutes had passed after we arrived, and I was already in love with the tranquility of the rural life. I somehow started to get some idea of why my grandparents refused to leave this serene place and move to Taipei with us.

Flickr, By: 陳良道 [https://www.flickr.com/photos/idisdao/14767565677]

After having some exploration by myself for a few days, I finally got the chance to experience what it was like to be a farmer with my family. I have seen some farmlands and orchards in Taipei before, but I never had any chance to really feel the softness of the soil with my barefoot and observe the crops in a close distance. Therefore, when we arrived at the potato farmland, I was surprised by the fact that the potatoes did not grow on the trees but was actually grown underground. For a city kid who never really had the chance to know nature, it was such an astonishing and revolutionary discovery.

For the next couple of hours my brother and I were busy fighting with the soil and struggling to use all of our strength to pull the potatoes out. For the first time in Tainan, I laughed so happily and so hard. For the first time, I did not care whether I would get dirty or not, whether my hands and white t-shirt would be covered with dirt or not. I was simply enjoying my afternoon with my family on this beautiful land. Before, I never bothered myself to understand anything about this island, but after all these fun and precious experiences, I started to really discover and, more importantly, cherish some of Taiwan's beauties that I had been ignoring for such a long time.

Flickr, By: 陳良道 [https://www.flickr.com/photos/idisdao/14767565677]

We had a fun and enjoyable day, but just when we were planning to head back home, hard rain started to pour down from the sky. All of us were shocked by this sudden change. The good news was that we did not have to walk back home carrying all the potatoes with us but the bad news was that the truck had no roof for us to hide from the rain. Except for my brother and the driver, the rest of us reached home with a body soaked wet. It may sound pretty bad, but it turned out to be the best memory from this trip. When other drivers passed by our convertible car, their stunned faces made my family and I laugh even louder. With all the water covering my eyes, the world started to become blurry but all the smiles on their faces were still as vivid and as beautiful as usual. Until now, even after so many years, I can still recall the same joy I felt under that pouring rain.

Although both were part of the island, Tainan and Taipei had gradually become two distinct regions that reflect their own lifestyle and uniqueness. It turns out that I like Tainan just as much as I like Taipei.

After all, Taipei is not my home, Taiwan is.

As the scene started to become blurry and then disappear, reality returns. However, I cannot stop to imagine what it would be like if China does take over Taiwan just like what they did decades ago to Hong Kong. Will Taiwan be the same? Will this beloved island of mine still be my home? I guess not. In every aspect, we are just too different to be the same. Even with an island as small as Taiwan can contain two distinct regions, how many differences can we possibly have as we compare Taiwan to China? And no, "one country, two systems" will not work. Just take a look at Hong Kong and the answer will be pretty obvious. 50 years of autonomy had been promised before the return. But what happens now? Elections are manipulated in favor of pro Chinese candidates. Freedom slowly slips through the hands of Hong Kongese. Sadly, under the cover of a prosperous financial center in Asia, this is the cruel reality of Hong Kong's current state.

It terrifies me when the thought of losing our rights of speech, universal suffrage, and freedom crawls in my mind. I grew up viewing these as our inalienable rights. This democratic government of ours has always been something that we Taiwanese people are proud of. It may not be the most effective system, but it is a symbol that represents our democracy, a land where all men's voices are heard. As the only democratic government in Chinese speaking country, this institution of ours is the backbone of the nation and what we are made of. If "returning" means giving up all these rights and our identities, then for sure we will defend our country as Taiwanese.

After all those protests I saw on the news, embarrassments we took, and the precious memories of this land I created with my friends and families, they culminated in an epiphany: I am proud of being a Taiwanese, even when it means that we will not be able to sing our national anthem in any international event. Even when it means that we will always be known as Chinese Taipei or Republic of China but never as Taiwan. Even when it means that we cannot take seats in UN. Even when it means that we will not be able to proudly wave our flags. Even when it means that we will continue to face the constant military and diplomatic pressure from our neighbor. Still, I am proud of being a Taiwanese, and always will be. I created many precious memories on this land. It is my root and where I belong. No matter how long the fight of gaining recognition will take, I know I will always stand up for it, just like how I stood up in the auditorium that day.